WOMEN TO  WALK WITH
SERIES

The WOMEN TO WALK WITH SERIES brings women out of the shadows of the Bible into contemporary relevance. For women seeking to reclaim the feminine voice in Scripture, these explorations of biblical women's stories go beneath the surface to probe the richness of their lives and relationships. But the exploration doesn't stop with the ancient record. The personal reflection questions at the end of each chapter invite readers to connect with Scripture in a personal way. Each chapter also includes discussion questions and exercises for a group study, making the WOMEN TO WALK WITH SERIES a valuable resource for church groups seeking biblical models for understanding women's experience.

Seasons of
Friendship

Other books by Marjory Zoet Bankson:

Braided Streams: Esther and a Woman's Way of Growing

The Call to the Soul: Six Stages of Spiritual Development

WOMEN TO WALK WITH
SERIES

Seasons of Friendship

Naomi and Ruth as a Model for Relationship

Marjory Zoet Bankson

Augsburg Books
MINNEAPOLIS

SEASONS OF FRIENDSHIP
Naomi and Ruth as a Model for Relationship

Large-quantity purchases or custom editions of this book are available at a discount from the publisher. For more information, contact the sales department at Augsburg Fortress, Publishers, 1-800-328-4648, or write to: Sales Director, Augsburg Fortress, Publishers, P. O. Box 1209, Minneapolis, MN 55440-1209.

Unless otherwise indicated, Scripture is taken from the Book of Ruth, the *Holy Bible, New International Version* ®, copyright © 1973, 1978, 1984 International Bible Society. Used by permission of Zondervan Publishing House. All rights reserved.

Scripture quotations marked NRSV are from the *New Revised Standard Version Bible*, copyright © 1989 by the Division of Christian Education of the National Council of the Churches of Christ in the USA. Used by permission.

Scripture quotations marked JB are from *The Jerusalem Bible,* copyright © 1966 by Darton, Longman & Todd, Ltd. and Doubleday & Company, Inc. Used by permission of the publisher.

Library of Congress Cataloging-in-Publication Data
Bankson, Marjory Zoet.
  Seasons of friendship : Naomi and Ruth as a model for relationship / by Marjory Zoet Bankson.—New rev. ed.
    p. cm.—(Women to walk with series)
  Includes bibliographical references and index.
  ISBN 0-8066-5136-9 (alk. paper)
1. Ruth (Biblical figure) 2. Naomi (Biblical character) 3. Friendship—Biblical teaching. 4. Bible. O.T. Ruth—Criticism, interpretation, etc. I. Title. II. Series.
  BS580.R8B36 2005
  222'.3506—dc22   2004023322

Cover design by Dave Meyer; cover art from Getty Images/Thinkstock. Used by permission. Book design by Michelle L. N. Cook

Manufactured in the U.S.A.

09   08   07   06   05   1   2   3   4   5   6   7   8   9   10

To Marianne Almer Johnson,
a friend in every season!

Contents

Acknowledgments

Few of us get the chance to rewrite a book after twenty years, so I am grateful to Augsburg Books for giving me that opportunity with this new edition of *Seasons of Friendship*.

That the story of Ruth and Naomi continues to yield new insights about friendship in different seasons of our lives tells me again that these women are living metaphors. After many years of leading women's retreats on various aspects of spiritual growth, I still think that women's friendship is the most important and least valued process for bringing the feminine capacity for feeling and empathy into our public life—as Ruth and Naomi did.

Rewriting the book has also given me a chance to look more closely at my friendship with Marianne Johnson over a longer period of time, to see how she has been both a companion and a goad to continue exploring those parts of my life that were largely unconscious. I am grateful that she is willing to let me tell what is really *our* story, a

Invitation

*E*very one of us longs to be known, understood, and received without conditions. But we live in a promiscuous culture in which the quiet support of committed friendship goes largely unnoticed—except for the shallow sitcom versions. We move from person to person, group to group, looking for a place to be loved. We search for a perfect mate, or we compromise ourselves in a harmful relationship, because we are afraid that no one can really accept the full range of who we are.

We imagine that marriage will ultimately fill our need for intimacy and companionship, only to discover that the burden is too great for one other person to carry. Some turn to a therapist, hoping to "fix" themselves or their mate. Others bail out of marriage when it fails to deliver the perfect partner, thinking their pain is caused by the relationship. In truth, it is neither. Rather, we are too complex for one partnership to contain. I thought that marriage would solve the problem—that Peter Bankson would be my closest friend for life. After more than forty years together, we are still "best friends," and yet I have discovered that different seasons in my life require different kinds of friendship and different levels of companionship. Because I am changing and dying and growing all the time, learning how to sustain long-term friendships is even more complex than finding an ideal mate.

If we have a primary relationship, too often time pressures cause us to ignore or compromise the very friendships that would provide a matrix of connections that would nourish a marriage or a specially-bonded relationship. Without friends, even our primary relationships lose their quality and resiliency because we fall into habits or patterns that might be challenged or changed by new friends. The friends who provide space for our individuality—and companionship for the loneliness created by that individuality—also provide a context for self-identity that is essential to being truly alive. Without friends, we lose touch with our humanity.

The trouble is that close friendships are hard to nurture and even harder to keep in our transient world. Most of us have learned more about losing friends by moving away than we know about finding new ones or about deepening the friendships we have. The emphasis on individualism and autonomy in our culture works against making sacrifices to maintain a valued friendship, but I believe God has planted a seed of longing to be known and understood that blooms into friendship if given half a chance. We can move beyond the sitcom versions of friendship and discover the rich hues of relationship that give our lives meaning in every season.

This book is about friendship and about being a friend, but there is no advice or easy formula here. Rather, I have taken the biblical story of Ruth and Naomi as a polarizing lens through which we can look at our lives as contemporary women. Through the story of these two ancient women, I hope to bring focus and clarity to some of the dynamics that assist or hinder friendship.

The connection between my own search for a close friend and the biblical story of Ruth began quite unconsciously. Like many other couples of our generation, Peter and I used Ruth's pledge to Naomi as the basis for our marriage vows. Because it was my role to shape the wedding ceremony, I chose Ruth's pledge as the ideal statement of my own intention: to let go of family and place as the reference for my identity and choose into our future together. As we turned from the altar, the minister read Ruth's promise:

> Where you go I will go,
> and where you stay I will stay.
> Your people will be my people
> and your God my God. (Ruth 1:16)

The statement was true for me then, and it still describes the core of my commitment to Peter, but the process of going and lodging and finding "my people," and discovering the nature of God, has been varied and difficult, rich and rewarding. The process has brought me back to the story of Ruth and Naomi with different eyes. I now see the biblical story as a story of friendship after the conventional supports of marriage and family are stripped away by death. It is a story of how two women began to experience God's presence in a way that gave them value and worth at a time when the culture regarded women as property and mere incubators for children. The Book of Ruth is also a parable of God with us in daily life, of God as friend.

Historically, the story is set in the period before David's monarchy, in the time "when the judges ruled" (1:1), about 1100 BC. Defined as a people by their monotheism and covenant relationship with Yahweh, the Hebrews had gained control of the highlands on the west side of the Dead Sea following their exodus from Egypt. Their God, Yahweh, was generally pictured as a male warrior and judge during that period.

Many biblical scholars agree that the Book of Ruth was actually written in the post-exile period of Ezra and Nehemiah (fifth century BC), when the issue of cultural and religious purity was part of re-establishing Israel's identity in their homeland. This was the period when the Torah was rediscovered and put into practice by reformers. Some authors say that Ruth was written to counter the campaign against marrying foreign women because it shows how God honored her decision to accompany Naomi. After living with this biblical story so closely, I believe that the Book of Ruth introduces another view of God who is more feminine and relational: nurturing, protective, and creative. That, too, is part of our biblical heritage, though it is not as well known or accepted.

In Jewish practice Ruth's story has been associated with the Feast of Weeks, which marked the spring grain harvest or the "first fruits" (Exodus 23:14-17, Exodus 34:22, Deuteronomy 16:9-12). The Feast of Weeks was also known as Pentecost because it was celebrated fifty days after Passover, as a remembrance of Moses receiving the law. Elements of Naomi's faith and Ruth's commitment echo Moses's faith and the Exodus story, although the female figures stand in shocking contrast in their courage and simplicity. Naomi and Ruth had no burning bush, no manna in the desert, no pillar of flame, and no promise of final security, yet they, too, undertook a desert journey toward the Promised Land.

Given the period and the patriarchal bias of fifth century Israel, it is startling to see God's presence and purpose embodied by these two women. Their friendship implies a larger purpose for women than bearing children and a more inclusive loving God than the Exodus story reveals. If Moses led a people to external freedom and identity, Naomi and Ruth lead us to an internal Promised Land of spiritual wholeness and integration. More like the New Testament understanding of Pentecost, the story of Ruth presents the Spirit behind the Law. I see a prophetic theme in Ruth, a theme that values women as people and opens the covenant to all people who are called to faith in God. Ruth presages the inclusive vision of *shalom* that Jesus lived five centuries later.

Friendship

The translation of Ruth's name provides a focus on friendship and a connection with the nature of God as friend. One source quotes the Hebrew root for Ruth, *rut*, as a contraction meaning "lady friend."[1]

Another identifies Ruth as a Moabite word connected with the verb *ra'ah*, meaning "shepherding a flock," denoting "to associate with" and connoting "friend or friendship."[2] Both sources point to friendship as the core of Ruth's name and, therefore, as the central theme in this story of Pentecost.

Since Pentecost has further been transformed by Christians—from a festival celebrating the receipt of the Law fifty days after Passover, into the coming of the Holy Spirit to the early church some fifty days after Easter—we can look at the story of Naomi and Ruth with new eyes. The notion of being able to connect at the heart level, to understand people who speak a different language, is the essence of Pentecost for Christians—and could be the definition of true friends as well. Even when we figuratively speak different languages, there is a heart connection that bridges those differences. I invite you to hold that thought as you begin to read and think about your friendships.

Your Mother's House

Early in the biblical story, after the death of her husband and two sons, Naomi pronounced a crucial command to her daughters-in-law, Ruth and Orpah: "Go back each of you to your mother's house" (1:8 NRSV). It was an invitation to them to return to the known territory of childhood and tradition in a matriarchal society, while she moved on toward an unknown future, beyond the safety of social rules and roles. When Ruth chose to go with Naomi, she left her "mother's house" forever.

At the beginning of every woman's spiritual journey is the decision to leave our "mother's house." It is the beginning of mature self-identity. We do it in layers, again and again. As we let Naomi's challenge resound inwardly, like Orpah we may need to go back to our "mother's house" because we are not ready to leave that primary field of identity as a woman, or because there is unfinished business to be completed. Some of us will examine the choice and decide, as Ruth did, that it is time to leave the past behind and make a commitment to friendship without knowing where it will lead. Some of us will have to stand in

Naomi's place, bereft of all past security, willing to risk everything for a rumor of hope that seems far away in the future.

Seasons

The image of "seasons" in friendship has emerged out of my reflections on the story of Naomi and Ruth. There is the obvious metaphor of beginning in famine and ending with the abundance of the grain harvest, but there are longer cycles hidden in this story as well. In nature we experience similarities in summers and winters, but each year has its own character. Sometimes the distinctions are subtle and softer, as in the Pacific Northwest where I grew up; sometimes the contrasts are extreme, as in Alaska where I lived when I was first married. Each season of friendship gives rise to new life for one or both partners, as it did for these biblical women. The overlay of nature and religious celebrations takes on additional meaning when we can find those same patterns in our own lives. The spiral of seasons provides an image of faith development that can reveal places where we are stuck or may have a special need. I hope that the metaphor of seasons will reveal some of the richness in the story of Naomi and Ruth, as well as in your own friendships.

Throughout the book I have included examples from my life as a model for ways in which you might find the spirit of these biblical women in your friendships. The questions "For Personal Reflection" at the end of each chapter are designed to help you reflect on your own life story through the lens of this one.

Sharing your answers to the journal questions with others in an attitude of prayer and openness can take the reflection process one step further toward healing the past and energizing the future. I hope you will consider using the guidelines "For a Group" at the end of each chapter for an eight-week course to build new friendships and a stronger fabric of personal relationships. By telling our stories, we can open our lives to God and to the community of other seekers. The process will gradually reach back in time, so we can learn to love those parts of our lives that seem unacceptable today. We can even learn to name and love our internal enemies, although we may never like them. I dream of a time when the churches on every corner can be a place for discovering friends to bless our lives with acceptance and interest, with commitment and support. In that company we can share the journey of faithful people everywhere.

Before you begin, take a few minutes and read the story of Ruth as it is found in any translation of the Bible.

expectations for marriage that popular culture suggests. Traditional images of marriage as a magical meeting of soul mates die hard, and many of them lie in wait for us in the kitchen and bedroom. We look for eternal spring with a marriage partner and are surprised when another season comes.

Single women, too, need mothering at the same stage of setting up a separate household. Often our own mothers are too far away, either physically or psychologically, to help much. Since the cultural ideal for both men and women today is autonomy or complete independence, then nothing really prepares us for the loneliness of leaving home or the tasks of creating community across generational lines.

As we have moved away from the unconscious communities of small-town America, we are left with little understanding and few tools to create community or develop friendships more intentionally. In our flight from churches and clubs, we have lost the volunteer associations that once brought contact with others in the same situation. My mother, for example, found her spring friends in a preschool study group sponsored by the American Association of University Women. Known as her "study club," it continued to be her primary circle of friends for more than fifty years! But today mobility and constant change work against finding a special friend who can companion us through the many transition times we will face.

As I look back at my early years of marriage, I am surprised by the similarity my story seems to have with Naomi's story. Peter and I were married soon after we graduated from college, and we moved to Alaska for his first army assignment. We are both eldest children from traditional families, with fathers who worked hard and mothers who stayed home. In Fairbanks our closest friends were two other young couples in exactly the same circumstances: The wives were teachers, and the husbands were lieutenants in different army units. I looked for supportive friends to fill the companionship void that my two younger sisters had filled when I was growing up. With them, I had learned to share successes and minimize failures at the family dinner table, to accept our differences, and to look out for each other. Loyalty was a high value in our family, and I had grown up feeling protective of my younger siblings, while sometimes wanting an older sister to take care of me. Now I realize that I carried those patterns into adult friendships with other women, especially at the beginning of a new cycle.

When the men were "in the field" for training, two or three of us would often get together to grade papers, read, knit, or just talk. We reached out for companionship and intellectual stimulation from each other, shared practical information and fun time, too, because we were so far from "home," that mythical place of warmth and welcome that we each held in our hearts. One to one, we shared some of the hardships and disappointments of married life, but generally we provided encouragement and emotional support for each other as spring friends.

Sharing food and drink is a Mother-Child equivalent of sexual intimacy, and I would say that most of us discovered that sex with a marriage partner was no substitute for the care and nurture we needed as we adjusted to marriage. Spring friends often gather around food, meeting for coffee at a favorite hangout or pooling leftovers for time together. Learning to cook and entertain others more informally than my mother did was a constant thread through my earliest round of spring friendships as we established our first home in a brand new place.

We need spring friends when we move into a new situation or take on a new challenge, when something new is being born in our lives. If we understand that all adults—men and women—go through periods of dependency and a need for emotional nurturing when a new stage or part of one's self is being born, then we do not have to be afraid of needing such care or offering it to others.

Summer: Season of "I"

With the same inevitability that the seasons in nature come around with the sun, internal or external changes take us from spring friendships into summer. Idealism gives way to practical realities, and we tire of the very things that once fed us. Individually, we begin to hunger for more autonomy and independence. Relationally, the cozy intimacy of "we" gives way to open spaces and different activities that help us achieve separate identities. An assertive "I" emerges.

As a result of our internal changes, we are drawn to summer friends whose characteristics differ from the mothering qualities we sought earlier. Summer friends are less nurturing, more distinct and functional, and more stimulating than spring friends. Sometimes abrasive and challenging, summer friends call forth initiative, individuality, and independence.

The shift from spring to summer for Naomi came slowly over several years as the juiciness of young motherhood in Bethlehem gave way to the hardened soil and sun-baked days of an unwanted summer season. Famine stalked the land and threatened the people of Israel with starvation. God seemed absent, and they felt abandoned.

Some stayed in Bethlehem, hoping for a sign of Yahweh's covenant promise of deliverance once again. Others left to look elsewhere for sustenance. When Elimelech and Naomi decided to leave the Promised Land, they also left the implied "we" of their covenant relationship with God. They decided to depend on their own resources rather than wait for a miracle. By leaving Bethlehem, they separated from past securities of land and people and God to establish control over their own lives.

Traveling away from their homeland in Judah, around the Dead Sea, Naomi and Elimelech headed eastward toward the land of Moab where food was thought to be more available. Mythically, they left the protective and nurturing promise of the covenant for an unknown future. Pared down to the bare essentials, they fled from the shadow of death, risking God's displeasure and rejection for their own survival. It was a powerful assertion of separation and individuality, of ego strength in the face of death. The young couple had to rely on their own wits and trust the presence of God to go beyond the laws and customs of their past because there was no earthly authority to provide them with safe passage. Their journey around the Dead Sea was symbolic of their choice for independence, for a summer relationship with God as well as with human friends.

When they arrived in Moab, Naomi had to find ways to make a new home in a foreign language among the Moabite women. That called for strength her mother had never needed, for skills she had never learned in Bethlehem. Somehow she was able to make that transition without the supportive network of the women who had mothered her in Bethlehem. She learned to stand on her own feet and trust her path.

Naomi and Elimelech succeeded in making a place in Moab, finding ways to live and work while both sons grew, but the difficulty and separateness of their life in Moab was symbolized by the fact that there were no more children. Elimelech's name conveyed his continuing allegiance to Yahweh, but there was no community to worship with, nobody to recall the stories of their faith or to encourage their determined autonomy. The unconscious communal context for their faith was gone.

As strangers in a strange land, the isolated Hebrew family probably continued their own religious practices within the household and remained aliens among the goddess worshipers of Moab. As Naomi toughened her pleasantness into purpose, she guarded her own brood. Survival and separateness clarified her character and defined her identity as a Hebrew woman alone in a foreign land. Yet Naomi must have found enough support during those long years in Moab to make it home to her. Her summer friends were those who could meet her strength with their own.

Leaving home and claiming the separateness of "I" from the fusion of a family marks the season of summer in our lives, too. We feel restless, unsatisfied, anxious. Old patterns no longer nurture us. Marriages dry into roles and routines. Jobs lose their challenge, and we begin to search the bookshelves for other people's stories to stretch our minds or disturb our souls. Summer light and heat drive us to change. For some, an internal summer season comes when children grow up and mothers begin to ask, "What's next?" At a later stage of life, summer comes internally when a career choice is completed or the time comes for retirement. Sometimes it is a body change that demands a psychic shift, and other times we notice dreams that signal the need for more challenge in the world. We may feel hungry or thirsty, even when there is enough literal food for sustenance. Indeed, we may try to fill that spiritual hunger with physical food and notice suddenly that we are gaining (or losing) weight as a sign that our souls are wanting a more unique identity.

Summer means finding a way to live in a strange new landscape, strengthening ego boundaries, and forging an inner will rather than depending upon approval from a mothering figure. A new form of "I am" emerges from the spring bonding of "we," tougher and more tenacious about claiming a separate self. Competition can be an important part of summer friendship, even when it manifests as envy or dislike. As a way of separating from one's family, we may choose a summer friend who would bring family disapproval for the way she looks or acts. As a way to discover how we are different from our parents, siblings, or life partner, we may choose a summer friend who mirrors our uniqueness and helps us leave behind the dependency that was so important before. Summer friends may also offer encouragement in a new situation, making a phone call or sending an e-mail at a critical time.

After two years of teaching in Alaska, I decided to go back to school for graduate study in history. I wanted something more to feed my soul than teaching eighth graders, but I was also ready for a new intellectual challenge. Perhaps, too, I had grown beyond my romantic dream that marriage would complete me without further inner work. (At that time I didn't even know such a thing as "inner work" existed!) My inner world dried out as a summer season unaccountably seared the landscape of early companionship with Peter. Nothing that I could put my finger on caused the shift; it simply happened.

Through a connection from my college roommate, I met a summer friend who was teaching economics at the University of Alaska. Her questions helped me find language for my opinions, and her presence validated an intellectual part of my life that had been submerged in the homey closeness of my spring friendships. This tall Jewish woman from New York City embodied difference in Fairbanks, challenging the values implied by Peter's army career with her anti-war remarks and, at the same time, inviting friendship out of her own loneliness. She was obviously different from me, and that helped me to identify my own boundaries, to experience myself as "I" instead of part of a "we."

With the deep connection that we had, I am sad to realize that I do not even know where she lives now. As a summer friend, we moved apart as our lives took different directions. She did not stay in my life as part of the circle of friends who have continued to sustain my sense of self. Perhaps summer friends are more likely to connect deeply and then slip out of our lives, like bees in the process of pollination, because they are not rooted in an ongoing community. Instead, summer friends are likely to be solitary figures who meet us at critical times of stretching boundaries and risking beyond the safe dyads of spring. Summer friends belong to a particular time and place, at the edge of one's known past, calling forth unique differences, righting the balance between pairing and person.

Autumn: Season of "Us"

In nature, autumn is the time to harvest what has been sown in the spring and ripened by summer sun. Whether bountiful or spare, fall harvest is a communal activity, a time of sorting and storing, celebrating with a cluster of people representing extended family. Autumn friends belong to whatever our tribe has become, to whatever group we consider "us." We join with them in the harvesting process and find nourishment in communal activities. A former spring friendship may suddenly mature as the nurturing qualities of a special twosome are spread out to include other people, or perhaps a singular summer friendship is integrated into one's community as the number of connections expand. If summer is a period of independence and search, then fall is a time of interdependence and storing away, a season to celebrate the richness of different people coming together—a season of "us."

For Naomi, autumn was marked by the death of Elimelech and her decision to stay in Moab rather than returning home to Judah. By the time her sons were grown, Naomi apparently felt at home in this foreign land, even though her comfort there must have been tested when her husband died. At that point, she might have returned to her homeland in Bethlehem in order for her sons, Mahlon and Chilion, to marry Hebrew women. Instead, she remained in Moab where her two sons married foreign women, Ruth and Orpah. Naomi's decision to stay was an affirmation of the community that she had found in Moab, no matter how different it was from her own religious tradition.

According to the biblical story, Naomi's autumn period lasted for ten years. Although the fruits of her life seemed meager—years passed and no grandchildren were born—Naomi did not weaken in her resolve or abandon her home in Moab. In this extended autumn season, Naomi's hope and faith lay with her living sons who could provide an economic base for the family and might also give her family a future, if they had children.

As the heart of her small family, Naomi was still very much identified with the role of being a mother, but her role had a different quality because she was also the head of her household. The names of her sons, which meant "sickness" and "pining away," suggest that Mahlon and Chilion were not strong male figures who could take over their father's role. Naomi discovered her stubborn strength, her inner resources for sustaining her family in a foreign land. Her autumn years were a time of consolidating her power, stabilizing her relationships with her daughters-in-law, and establishing her own kind of spiritual leadership within the family.

As the years went by, Naomi's family would have developed a sense of "us" as separate from the society in which they lived. To sustain her hope, Naomi probably returned to some of the roles and traditions that had sustained her when she first moved from her mother's home: finding community in the shared tasks of women's work and comfort in the stories of the Exodus, Passover, and God's provision of food and water as the Israelites lived in the desert between Egypt and the Promised Land.

As a seasonal metaphor, autumn is a time of harvest. If there has been enough rain to balance summer's heat and light, then autumn brings abundance, plenty of food, and celebration rituals for a whole community in thanksgiving. If there has not been enough water and food is scarce, the drought of summer creates an element of fear about survival through the coming winter, and autumn friends cluster around, parceling out scarce resources. This is true inside as well as out, in our souls as well as in nature. When the individual work of summer has brought good results, autumn is a time of communal celebration. When results are meager, as they were for Naomi, autumn is a time of pruning and paring down.

Autumn friends thrive in the context of ritual community, whether we invite it around the dinner table or join an established group or a larger cluster of people with a spiritual or sacred dimension, such as a social action committee or a church. We may seek community by returning to the customs and rituals of our parents. Autumn friends can give us a sense of being grounded where we are, or they may simply be a group of people who gather in one place for a common activity but do not know one another. We may even turn to the pseudo-community of television because it does not demand that we deal with real people who have different customs.

The simple fact of language suggests that humans are created for community and for communicating with each other. We begin to find community in a new place by returning to or creating a common body of rituals and interpretive stories with others who are different from us but share the same place or resources. Community values, rituals, customs, and traditions provide a context of meaning for the joys and sorrows that come to all of us.

For some, autumn friends make an extended family; for others, a sacred community; for still others, a network of individuals spread across the country who can be supportive by phone, e-mail, and an occasional visit. Those autumn friends, whose words touch something deeper than the surface level of cooperation, become part of our interpretive framework as we learn the deeper lessons of caring for those who are not like ourselves.

In our first cycle of seasons as adults, Peter and I looked for autumn community among the people who clustered around our special interests beyond work: books and conversation, skiing and photography. Because we had both come from intact extended families, we expected holidays to be family affairs, but we were too far from home to go back. Instead, we tried to create community around our dinner table by inviting diverse friends from the university and the army post. At Christmas and Easter, we made a special effort to include others who might also be feeling lonely and far from home. For an evening, at least, we could share the harvest of our lives and feel a sense of belonging to something larger and more lasting—a ritual community, a season of "us."

As my spring and summer friends moved away from Alaska, and graduate school shifted my focus from teaching to learning, I reached out to a new community of friends who shared my interests at the university. One special friend emerged from the cluster of couples whom we saw regularly. Ann was in a book club with me, and we deepened our friendship when she became the editor of a small literary magazine for which I was writing. Her interests and education were similar to mine, and when each of our mothers visited Alaska, she and I found some additional background connections. Although our relationship was not as intense as my earlier spring pairings, she is still part of my support network after more than forty years, while the others are not. Perhaps an autumn friendship is more likely to persevere because it thrives in a matrix that is complex and interpretive, less personal and more archetypal. Autumn friends are more likely to stay in touch, sending Christmas cards and address changes, because they are rooted in more traditional patterns of community.

Winter: Season of "Me"

The transition from autumn to winter usually comes with a crisis, descending like a sudden freeze. When winter comes as a season of friendship, we move away from others and go deep inside to focus on "me." Like hibernating animals, we burrow within ourselves and withdraw from more "friendly friends," choosing those who will walk with us in silence. Winter is a time for solitude and commitment to inward leadings.

The close of Naomi's autumn years were marred by the bitter realization that her childless sons carried some kind of curse: Even their names—"sickness" and "pining away"—suggested illness or blight. With no sign of children, there may have been increasing alienation from the fertility-worshiping culture in Moab. Autumn faded into winter as Naomi's two sons sickened and died. She was an old woman with no one to protect or care for her. Like many women who identify themselves solely with the role of being wife and mother, Naomi considered her life finished. It looked as if Yahweh had abandoned her in a foreign country and, by cursing her family with barrenness, had stripped away the only promise of life after death that these ancient cultures recognized.

Then Naomi heard that God had visited her own people in Bethlehem, bringing food. Frozen with grief and stoic in the face of her losses, she set her face toward her homeland. Although the external signs of life were negative, Naomi was able to take this act of will and of faith. Her decision grew out of the independence she had gained during her summer years in Moab and the spiritual consolidating she had done during her autumn period. She had faith that God would not turn against her if she went back.

With Ruth and Orpah alongside her, Naomi started for Bethlehem on foot. She had come full circle, retracing the journey she had made with Elimelech from Bethlehem to Moab so many years before. But this time, Naomi had two mature daughters-in-law with her, and there was no man for comfort or protection. The three widows walked westward around the Dead Sea, a stark reminder of their situation. Wrapped in silence, they moved slowly away from Moab toward Bethlehem without any guidance except Naomi's memory and her will. The promise of food was hope enough to feed Naomi's soul as her sturdy feet plodded across the desert, one step at a time. Though traveling with others, Naomi was essentially alone in the winter season of her life.

Death, literal or figurative, marked the shift into winter friendships for Naomi as it does for many of us today. Winter comes when we turn from extroverted relationships in community to an introverted focus on self and survival. It can happen when an important relationship or community is suddenly taken away, as it was for Naomi. It can happen through a change in health or economic circumstances, job, or home setting. Winter withdrawal may also happen simply because we are creatures sensitive to darkness and light, cold and warmth, and our souls need a time to rest and renew from the inside out. It is a season when the fields lie fallow, soaking up the energy for another cycle of growth. Winter friends wait together, connecting in silence around some small source of warmth or hope.

For Peter and I, winter came when we moved from Alaska to Georgia because of Peter's army career. Leaving graduate school was a severe blow to me, shattering the community I had found at the university. My coursework was done, comprehensive exams passed, but my thesis was not yet completed. It would take five more years and as many moves to finish that final piece. I also hated to leave the variety of friends we had gathered in Fairbanks during our three years there.

When we arrived in Georgia, my autumn friend, Ann, was there for a yearlong school assignment, which both our husbands had received. Her presence cushioned the pain I was feeling, and we did some things together. But that year I also turned inward and began a serious exploration of my faith. Questions replaced answers, and I felt unsure about myself, wondering whether I could finish the degree program I had started in Alaska and what the future might hold. In addition, the specter of Peter being sent to Vietnam, and the separation that would bring, loomed closer. Now I realize that I did not know how to share my feelings very well, so I lapsed into silence.

In the middle of that year in Georgia, our husbands both received orders to go to Vietnam after further training. Ann and I plunged deeper into a winter season of silence, chilled by apprehension about the future. When the year in Georgia ended and our husbands prepared to leave, she and I moved to different parts of the country to be near family, she to New Jersey and I to Washington state. We agreed to call each other once a month, just to stay in touch during the lonely year ahead. The promise of sharing my fears and hopes with a friend who would be enduring a winter season like mine sustained me as I moved away from the supportive community of other "waiting wives."

The Circle of Seasons

What we bring to any friendship is, first of all, the season in which we find ourselves. The cycle can take many years or a few short months. We may find ourselves in several of these seasons at once, claiming friends in each season to support different aspects of our lives. More likely, we will find ourselves with a spring friend in the midst of an autumn cluster of friends, or we will sense a summer/winter polarity without much nurture or community. What we have in common with the biblical story of Naomi and Ruth is that we will live through different seasons of life along with changing family demands—and always have the need for women friends beyond what a spouse can offer.

Also, because women live longer than men, most of us will need to find new friends as we age. My mother, in her late eighties, fell and broke her arm. Her sudden disability (she could not feed or dress herself) prompted a move from Washington State to Colorado so she could live near my youngest sister. Hampered by limited mobility and hearing problems, she is nevertheless faced with finding a new circle of friends so she will not be totally dependent on family for her social life. She is facing that challenge with the same grit and courage that Naomi exhibited when she left Moab. As my mother is teaching me with her life, the circle of seasons will continue as long as we live.

For Personal Reflection

Spring: Season of "We"

- When and where did you establish your first home?
- Did you have a close woman friend who shared that experience with you? How would you describe her?
- What kinds of things did you do together that felt nurturing?
- How did she help you value some new stage or phase of your life?

Summer: Season of "I"

- Identify a period in your life when you shifted from spring to summer.
- What prompted the shift in yourself? Was it internal or external, or both?
- Name a friend who shared that summer season of search, hungering, or new definition of yourself.
- How did this summer friend differ from your spring friend? How did your summer relationship differ from your spring relationship?

Autumn: Season of "Us"

- Identify the first community where you felt like an adult participant. Was that community clustered around your work? Home or church? A special interest?
- Did you have a particular woman friend in that community? Who was she and what did you do together?
- How was your relationship helped or hindered by your community?

Winter: Season of "Me"

- Remember the first time you left a community that was important to you.
- Where did you go and why? What resources sustained you?
- Describe a winter friend. What qualities of friendship are important to you during this season?

You can anchor these reflections in your journal by drawing your own circle of friendships. Divide your circle in fourths and label each quarter: winter, spring, summer, autumn. In each season, add the name of the friend you have identified in each season above, knowing that you may change her to another season later on. (If you plan on using the group suggestions on the next page, wait until your group gathers to draw your circle of friendships.)

For a Group

If you are going to share these exercises with a small group, be clear about the time, place, and regularity of your meetings. I suggest a group of six to twelve people who can meet weekly for 90 minutes.

(20 minutes)

Begin each session with a ritual of spreading a cloth or scarf to create an altar and lighting a candle. Open with some kind of ritual greeting, which may include a saying a prayer, singing, chanting a blessing together, or simply offering a period of quieting silence. Then read the poem that begins the chapter you will be using for that session. Whatever you do, it will signal the beginning of a sacred circle.

At this first session, the leader should bring four small objects that represent to her each of the four seasons (such as a bulb for spring, sunglasses for summer, a small basket for fall, and a bare branch for winter) and be prepared to say something about the underlying pattern of this biblical story of friendship as it is found in nature. Then read aloud the poem at the beginning of chapter 1: "The Circle of Seasons," stopping after each season to lay your object on the cloth or scarf and say why you chose that symbol.

(10 minutes)

Have paper and pens available for participants and give these directions:

To begin our life together as a group, we will take a few minutes of silence to each draw our own circle of friendships. Divide your circle in fourths and label each quarter: winter, spring, summer, autumn.

In each season add the name of a friend whom you think of, knowing that you may change her to another season later on.

(40 minutes)

To build a healthy group, you will want to begin with some clear ground rules for sharing (such as, "Don't give advice; share time equally; be personal; hold confidences in the group"). Then number off or simply ask people to move into triads for sharing, stating that they will change groups at each session so people will have a chance to be with everyone at some point.

Ask each person to describe a spring friendship to their triad. Suggest that this will be a chance to share some personal history and a time of "new beginning" with the group.

(20 minutes)

About 20 minutes before your closing time, call the triads back together and offer each person a chance to say one thing she learned or realized from today's session.

Ask the group to read chapter 2 for next week and bring with them a symbol of winter friendship for the altar.

Close with a silent or spoken prayer and extinguish the candle as a sign that the circle is ended.

Pay attention to beginning and ending on time—it is a way to build trust!

Chapter 2

Winter Friendship:
Finding My Self

Widows walking
grouped in grief
servants of custom;
not yet friends . . .

Naomi stopped. "Go back!
Return to your mother's house!"

One did.
Orpah ("turning away")
went back
to reverse the sun,
become a bride again.

One didn't.
Ruth ("beloved")
left her mother's house in Moab
choosing Naomi's way.

Did she leave
because she was loved?
Or because she was not?
Did she trust herself first?
Or Naomi's God?

Paired by Ruth's choice
Naomi and Ruth walked together
toward
. . . rumors of food and a future.

*T*he pattern of seasons in Ruth and Naomi's friendship began to unfold with their perilous journey back to Bethlehem. The earlier form of their relationship depended on roles and responsibilities in the family, but when the death of Naomi's two sons eliminated that structure, the women were plunged into a winter season that tested each to the core. Naomi, Ruth, and Orpah had to let go of the old structure and find a deeper sense of self in order to create something new together. Death was the crucible in which their winter friendship, the season of "me," began to form.

Naomi: Choosing Independence

When we face choices that will upset old relationship patterns that have sustained us, we need friends outside the system to companion us on the way. A crisis can open the psyche and also open our patterns of relationship to someone with a new vision of "how it could be." A winter friend may be an old friend who is also undergoing major change in her life, or it may be someone entirely new, someone who shares some part of the emerging pattern. These friends are given as a gift, undeserved and unearned: They are grace in winter.

For Naomi, death precipitated a kind of independence that set her apart from the dominant culture of her day. When her sons died, the economic base for the family in Moab was suddenly gone. Even if her sons had owned land, there were now no male family members to defend Naomi's claim to their property. And without land, the older woman and her two daughters-in-law had no economic options except begging or prostitution. As an old woman with no experience in making public decisions, Naomi might have crumpled into depression—but then there would be no story.

Instead of fading into the background, Naomi acted to claim their right to life when she decided that the three widows should take their chances and make the long journey back to Bethlehem. There she had some hope for survival, even if the trip itself was extremely dangerous. Yahweh was said to have visited the Hebrews and provided them with food again, bringing an end to the long famine that had originally driven Naomi and Elimelech away. Naomi knew that, unlike many other peoples of the ancient world, the Israelites allowed widows to glean in the fields after harvest, so she could imagine that they could find enough food to survive. She was ready to move toward that rumor of hope.

The younger women, Ruth and Orpah, had no choice. They belonged to Naomi by tribal custom, if not by law. No longer innocent or easily married again, Ruth and Orpah prepared to leave their home and families, native language and religious customs, to go with Naomi. Their journey would retrace Naomi's journey some twenty years earlier, but with no promise of children to give them a future, their prospects were dismal at best. They were simply choosing survival.

The three widows set out together, but then Naomi turned to the two younger women and directed them to leave her: "Go back each of you to your mother's house" (1:8 NRSV). Her words stopped the simple flow of the story, turning custom back on itself. Then she added, "May the Lord show kindness to you, as you have shown to your dead and to me" (1:8). She extended her spiritual authority and gave them God's blessing in response to their faithful service in her home.

Although Naomi felt abandoned and unblessed herself, she spoke from a position of authority as matriarch and spiritual head of the family. Stripped of external security, Naomi claimed a strength her story only hinted at before. In the eyes of Naomi's religious tradition, she and her husband had been disobedient by leaving the land promised by God to the Hebrew people. Still, she dared to call down God's blessing on her daughters-in-law because they, as foreign women, had been kind! Somewhere inside herself, Naomi discovered her grounding in God's spirit, and out of her wintry solitude she spoke from a place of strength and clarity.

As Naomi claimed the freedom to send Ruth and Orpah back to their own mothers, she, too, stood at a turning point, empty and yet determined. When she directed the young women to return to their homeland, she was making a statement of her independence: She was no longer willing to be the surrogate mother for them. She was ready to leave her role as wife and mother forever. As she directed them to leave, Naomi let go of their kindness, their dutiful support, and whatever form of friendship they had provided for her.

Seasoned by tragedy and enlivened by her own stubborn faith, Naomi was ready to walk the dangerous road toward Bethlehem by herself. Her decision marked the transition from identifying herself as a mother to being an independent person without family ties. She no longer identified herself with the childbearing capacity she once had. With sardonic humor she said to the younger women, "Return home, my daughters; I am too old to have another husband. Even if I thought there was still hope for me—even if I had a husband tonight and then gave birth to sons—would you wait until they grew up? Would you remain unmarried for them?" (1:11-13).

Naomi's hyperbole sketched the desperation of their situation. Time was short, prospects dim. Ruth and Orpah had to act to save themselves because Naomi could not. Outwardly, Naomi confronted each of the younger women with a choice. Inwardly, she must have been wrestling with her own questions about the future as they walked. She must have felt the weight of custom and responsibility for Ruth and Orpah. When she made her decision to send them back to their mothers, Naomi let go of whatever identity she may have felt in their dependence on her. She chose to focus on her self and her own needs; she was acting as a winter friend to herself!

As women, we are encouraged from birth to think first of our relationships to others and not to stand alone. We are programmed to think of ourselves as spring and autumn friends: nurturing, caring, and supportive toward others, men and women. We do not grow up with the expectation that we will have to be economically or socially or spiritually self-sufficient, even though feminism has certainly encouraged women in that direction, but women are not expected to be loners.

Our economic and social system encourages dependence for women because they are still the primary caregivers for children and for men. Yet most women will indeed spend a significant portion of adult life alone—by choice, widowhood, or divorce. Like Naomi, when suddenly released from conventional relationship structures, we may experience independence as a burden rather than an opportunity. As winter comes to each of us, we need to discover the inner resources to walk alone in the world. Yet our society offers many substitutes for the spiritual toughness and independence that a winter season demands.

In one sense, winter always requires that we choose independence. Because it is the season of dying and barrenness, of endings, stillness, and solitude, we must confront our mortal limits and let go of the wish-dreams that keep us bound to the past. Winter is a season of pruning, of letting go. It is a bodily experience of dying and must be mourned in order to discover the faint heartbeat of a new truth.

Naomi confronted the end of her sexual capacity to bear children and acknowledged that she did not see any further usefulness in her body, but she still wanted to live. From her inner resources, Naomi was able to move beyond the cultural definition of meaning for a woman's life to find a new level of purpose. She acted out of the startling assertion that God's provision of food for the Hebrews was also meant for her!

Spiritual growth always requires some kind of death, letting go of an old ego form or habitual pattern to let "me" and "my needs" emerge as the referent for decision making. Winter comes largely unbidden, through a personal crisis or shift in health, sometimes announcing its arrival with disturbing dreams or explosive anger. Even positive changes, such as marriage, becoming a mother, receiving a promotion, or retiring, can bring on a winter season for the soul because they bring loss of a former role or persona. But when we can move into it as Naomi did—resolute and stubborn in pursuit of life at the core—winter can be seen as a fallow field, full of promise with hidden seeds of hope.

I realize that I am always watching for winter-weathered women: seasoned crones who have lived beyond "pleasant" and "nice" to deal with harder things, who will speak up for themselves and others. They live close to the bone. Often they have grown beyond their biological families to care about issues of justice, and they have learned to savor little things that bring joy in the present moment. I notice women with gray hair and hard-earned wrinkles who are living full and interesting lives by themselves, whether they share space with others or not.

Among my seasoned friends, one is a particular model for me. During the years that she nursed her dying husband, Virginia took a course at the community college so she could build furniture and redecorate her house—doing all the work herself. Once her husband died and her daughters married, she began to travel to Asia whenever she could afford it. Between trips, she learned more about where she was going by immersing herself in the culture: food, friends, music, language courses, and books. She joked that she was "creating insurance" for her old age. Neither sentimental nor romantic about life in China, Vietnam, or Burma, she had enormous respect for the ways in which people in another culture build a coherent life. Her stories and pictures included the practical arts of clothing and furniture, diverse ways of earning money, details of family life, and the scope of religious rituals. Virginia's lively independence has given me a model for how to be a friend to myself and has made growing older very attractive for me.

Orpah: Choosing Dependence

When confronted with the choice to go back to their mothers' homes, both Orpah and Ruth initially protested and stated their intention to continue the journey with Naomi. Without any training or experience in making independent decisions for themselves, the choice to leave Naomi and return to their mothers must have been terrifying for them. Naomi was not only releasing them, but she was abdicating her role as caretaker and decision maker. As an archetypal Crone, Naomi was ready to cut her ties with the past and live with the consequences. Death had become her friend and ally, freeing her to act for herself and no one else.

After protesting Naomi's choice, Orpah kissed her mother-in-law and turned away, returning to her own mother in Moab. The young widow went back toward girlhood, not ready to leave the protection of home and family. Although her prospects for finding a husband were not very good—since she had been married to a foreigner and produced no children—she believed in her past more than she dared to believe in Naomi's future. Her marriage had been an extension of her own mother's nurture and guidance, and Orpah made a clear choice to look for more of the same by seeking a husband among the known patterns of her past. She wanted the familiar role of a wife more than she wanted to claim her independent power as a woman, so she settled for dependence and departed from the story. There is no condemnation of Orpah. She simply made a choice that cost her place in the larger drama of God's revelation through two ordinary women. Her role was to be the contrast, the "road not taken."

On the surface, Orpah's choice was logical. She continued to be a dutiful daughter-in-law by obeying Naomi. For her, the journey around the Dead Sea toward Bethlehem meant death because it meant giving up the dream of having a husband and children. Naomi was quite clear about the limitations that the return to Bethlehem would impose on Ruth and Orpah: Naomi could not provide the young women with husbands from Elimelech's family. Orpah simply did not have the inner resources to choose the risk of this unknown path.

Like Orpah, many women try to avoid the responsibilities of independence that come with divorce, with the death of a spouse, or with another major relational shift, such as children leaving home. Particularly if we have grown up with the dual expectation that marriage is essential for happiness, and that childbearing is critical to female fulfillment, we are likely to meet the prospect of living alone with despair, seeking refuge within the shelter of a biological family or a similar protective social grouping, such as a church or synagogue. We settle for dependence and wait for someone to rescue us.

Friendships that are embedded in the social fabric where we live may serve to keep us in dependent or even abusive relationships. Well-meaning autumn friends who connect in community can drain away the willpower needed to break with old patterns and set out toward Bethlehem, as Naomi did. We live in a culture that values comfort, offers many distractions, and provides pseudo-community or addictions to soothe our troubled minds when winter reaches out a hoary hand to drag us into a Dead Sea journey. Often it takes a therapist or spiritual director to hear the deep tides at work in the soul, inviting us to grapple with the independence demanded by a winter season, instead of escaping from it.

I made Orpah's dependent choice when I was twenty six and had been married for five years. Peter had received orders to go to Vietnam for the first time, and I had to decide where to live and what to do. At first, I thought that I would continue my college dreams of working in Washington, D.C., as a part of some political or legal office. But then, when I imagined what might happen inside of me if Peter were killed, I decided to return "to my mother's house." I called my parents in Bellingham, Washington, and asked them to find me an apartment near their home so I could be in a supportive environment. Like Orpah, I wanted to get away from the pain of winter. I returned to the community of my childhood to wait for Peter to come back. The ambition and self-confidence of my college and university years ebbed away in the fears that Peter would be killed or taken prisoner, and I was too frightened to walk alone. I was not free to choose for my *self* yet.

When I went back to Bellingham, I did discover new resources in an old community. An older couple, friends of my parents, offered me a place in which to work with clay and a potter's wheel. Every night, after I was finished teaching at the junior high, I went to Louie Mideke's studio where I worked alone, learning from my mistakes and asking questions when I needed help. His searching spirit was everywhere: in the handmade tools, careful records of glazes and firings, and his clay work on the shelves. At first, I was a harsh judge of my beginning efforts. Then gradually, I learned to love the work itself: the feel of clay, the rhythm of the wheel, the craft of making pots that sang after firing. That winter season became a time to focus on my *self* and my own needs, a time for solitude and discovering internal resources. The Midekes were winter friends who left me alone in a sheltered spot to discover internal resources I did not know I had. Sometimes that is the fortunate outcome of making Orpah's choice for dependence.

David Yohn, the pastor at the UCC Church in Hanover, made the church a safe place to experience the winter in my soul because he was adamant that we not make each other into symbols of war or peace while at church. On a church retreat, I found a winter friend who could walk with me. Joanne and I had never spoken about things that mattered deeply until we roomed together at a retreat led by the Ecumenical Institute of Chicago. The intense and structured environment gave us an opportunity to discover the thinking/wondering/searching selves behind the roles that had kept us apart, polite, and distant.

After Peter left for Vietnam, Joanne made a commitment to "be family" for me: She included me for family dinner twice a week, and she was willing to walk with me into the darker places of my fears when I was willing to name them. I often sat with Joanne and her family in church, where the rituals and prayers gave me space to grieve for lost dreams and face the reality of my life without Peter.

I learned something about interdependence that year. Joanne made it clear that we each brought something different to our friendship. As a mother with two young daughters, she offered me a home and family. As a college faculty member, I offered her conversation and ideas in areas that were not being encouraged in her role as a mother. And we both shared a lively interest in theology. Our reciprocal contributions to the friendship made my winter journey a time of self-discovery rather than self-pity.

Ruth and Naomi: Sharing Interdependence

Winter friendships require a certain level of independence to weather this season of solitude. The nurturing aspect of spring is missing; the stimulation of summer seems far away; and the comfortable camaraderie of autumn is replaced by the painful need for each one to take care of herself and simply be present to the other. Small gestures of tenderness may be enough to assure the other that you care. Like porcupines, winter friends show love carefully, often at a distance from one another.

The winter friendship of Ruth and Naomi began in silence as they walked together toward Bethlehem. Like time-lapse photography, the story simply reports that "the two women went on until they came to Bethlehem" (1:19). But human relationships take place in time and space, and Ruth's commitment must have been tested a hundred times on that long trip. Naomi's willingness to have Ruth with her must have been tested as well.

Naomi had already asserted her independence: She had been prepared to make the journey by herself and even to die, if that came to pass. Ruth also asserted her independence: She was ready to take responsibility for her own decisions, to set her own priorities, and to commit her time and energy. Each, therefore, was able to make a decision from the core of herself about the nature of their relationship. Sr. Joan Chittister points out in her book *The Story of Ruth* that "Independence gives a person a right to opt into the creation of community, not the responsibility to be used by the community for its own ends only."[4] That is, Naomi and Ruth could choose to be interdependent without losing themselves in the process.

A woman's journey must include these winter seasons of solitary determination in order to achieve the kind of detachment and ego strength that it takes to explore the full range of choices that we have. Ego strength in women has often been criticized as a masculine trait, but we recognize and respect women who know themselves well enough to make hard decisions and carry through with their commitments. Ruth's pledge is an example of that kind of ego strength—not rigid or doctrinaire, but one based on a living relationship with Naomi. The difficulty, it seems to me, is how to keep the ego permeable enough so love can take the lead. Ruth's promise embraced a wider grounding in the monotheism of Israel, so she was not trapped by the approval of Naomi or her particular personality. Ruth's statement was a covenant of grace with an open future.

For me, each time we moved because of Peter's army career, I felt a winter season in my soul. I lost whatever community I had managed to connect with and felt the loss of particular friends even more keenly. It happened seventeen times in twenty-one years. Each time it was a little death experience, capped by a "last supper" with friends we might never see again. I learned to speak my gratitude for friendship and support, and to share bread and wine as symbols of physical separation and ongoing spiritual connection. Our religious tradition provided a dinner table ritual with sacred overtones.

In each new place, after I had hung the curtains and found a grocery store, I would plant a rose bush because it was symbolic of my grandmother's home and permanency. I found that the only way I could walk through each wintry season was to plant my feet and send down rose roots, as though I would never move again. It was the only way I could be open to the gift of new relationships, new friends. My tendency was to stay closed, to protect myself from winter, because we might be moving again soon. But I soon realized if I did that, I would keep myself from the very friends who could sustain my sense of self in a new place.

As I approached the age of forty, we faced yet another move, this time from Leavenworth, Kansas, to Washington, D.C. I was plunged into a wintry season that seemed deeper because of my age. It felt like my last chance for children or a meaningful career. In Kansas, I had attended a few Faith@Work events and felt excited about their biblical and theological integration, which included physical, emotional, and relational dimensions of faith development. After we moved to Washington, D.C., I was asked to be on a leadership team for a week-long Faith@Work training event in Michigan. I could not believe my good fortune! It was like being pulled out of a wintry whirlpool and given another chance.

When I got to the retreat center, I discovered that all six leaders, men and women, were in some kind of transition at work or at home. Early in the week, we did an exercise in which each person had to identify three things they would save from a house fire . . . and then choose one of the other team members to receive those things. Intuitively, I chose Marianne because I sensed she would interpret my precious photo albums rightly. I trusted her with my life story even though we hardly knew each other at that point. The exercise put me in touch with the dangers and despair of such an imagined tragedy, and I surprised myself in choosing Marianne as a winter friend.

Later that week, I stumbled into Marianne's wintry soul space. My journal records it this way:

> . . . deep sobs in the bathroom . . . I went in, afraid of what I might see. M was gripping the sink, crying from her belly with her head against the mirror. Put my arm around her and felt her sag. "Would you hold me?"
>
> "Yes." Felt terrified. Went to my room . . . held her while she cried and cried. In bits and pieces the story came—her fourth child died in childbirth on this day ten years before. She had almost bled to death. When she "came to," the child was gone, unnamed and unknown. She had buried the memory to get on with her life . . . gotten sick at this time each year. Now this. What can I do?

Our friendship took a turn with Marianne's grief and my response. Our connection was at a level deeper than words. The intensity of her emotion was frightening and holy at the same time. Earlier in the week, I had seen only the responsible elder sister and the playful child in her. Now there was no escape into easy banter, and I could not ignore the depth of what we had shared: the risk of her trust in my stability and my vulnerability. I was able to walk through my fears and be present to her memory of losing a child and nearly losing her own life as well. Even though I could not identify with her experience, I discovered courage and responsiveness I did not know I had. Later, she said that my physical presence, without judgment or advice, had provided safety and space for her memories to surface.

Synchronously, both Marianne and I were scheduled to give workshops at her denominational gathering of women the following week, so we roomed together there for another "incubator" experience. As a nurse and psychologist, her workshop was titled "Say Good-Bye So You Can Say Hello," and it was about the necessity of grieving our losses in order to open psychic space for new life. She gave as an example her experience the previous week, and she began to make plans for some way to mark that child's life. I was at the conference with my potter's wheel, speaking about the inward and outward pressures that create the container of our lives, so I offered to make some kind of a container for whatever she would choose to symbolize this child's life. We then made a commitment to meet again on the anniversary of his death to complete a ritual of release. Rooming together at this church conference, where our only responsibility was to give our separate workshops, provided us with time to talk, to bond, and to bring our winter selves into relationship without the normal responsibilities that each of us had back home. I now realize what a gift that was.

Winter friendship often begins with a crisis and plunges both parties into some form of mutual vulnerability. The usual masks we wear in polite company are stripped away, and we meet at the level of raw need, which feels like survival even when that is not literally the case. It feels like "me" and "my needs" are paramount. What marks a winter friendship apart from a kind of crisis camaraderie is what happens next. If there is a context for learning and growing over time, two people who come together in a crisis can get to know the reality of the other person and develop a healthy interdependence and intimacy. Without such a context, they are likely to be "emergency room acquaintances" without a future together.

For Personal Reflection

Naomi: Choosing Independence

- Draw a timeline of your life, in any shape you want. You might divide it into four segments and identify a high point and a low point in each quarter.
- Mark the major events with a symbol and a date.
- Look at your timeline and mark the winter seasons when you walked alone as Naomi did with an **I** (for independence).
- What gift have you received from those times?
- How have you learned to be a friend to yourself?

Orpah: Choosing Dependence

- Mark your timeline with a **D** (for dependence) for the times when you made a choice for the familiar patterns of the past.
- How old were you? What were the circumstances?
- How did you make your choice?
- Where did you go? Who were your friends there?
- What did you learn about yourself?

Ruth: Choosing Interdependence

- Mark your timeline with a **T** (for interdependence) for the times when you felt both vulnerable and strong at a particular turning point.
- What or who enabled you to make the freer choice?
- Have you ever felt a commitment "until death," either to yourself or to another person?
- If so, what does that commitment mean to you now?

Ruth and Naomi: Sharing Interdependence

- Mark your timeline with the name of someone with whom you have shared a winter friendship.
- How has your relationship with this person grown and changed over time? What symbol could you add to symbolize this winter friend?

For a Group

(15 minutes)

When you meet for the second week, begin with the ritual of gathering that you have established. Spread a cloth or scarf for the altar and light the candle. Open with a prayer, a song, a chant, or a period of quieting silence. Then read the poem that begins this chapter. Invite each person to place her symbol of winter friendship on the altar cloth, saying a few words about why she chose this symbol.

Suggest that the group is creating an intentional community by sharing symbols and stories, letting each other know how we have lived through some winter seasons in our lives.

(10 minutes)
Use the poem to review the three types of winter friendship: Naomi's sturdy independence, Orpah's cautious return, and Ruth's daring choice into the unknown.

Encourage people to choose one winter season and a particular winter friendship to explore in depth during the sharing time. (Remind them once again of the guidelines for sharing. See pages 40-41.)

(45 minutes)
Ask the group to form triads with people different from the previous session. Invite each person to describe a winter friendship and how it began. Offer these questions for consideration:

- Have you ever made a one-sided commitment to someone else?
- What independence was required for each person?
- How did you share communication at a level deeper than words?
- What were some of the tensions in your relationship? Some of the gifts?

(20 minutes)
Return to the whole circle. Invite each person to retrieve her symbol of winter friendship from the altar and to speak briefly of something she learned about winter friendship during this session.

Ask the group to read chapter 3 for next week and bring with them a symbol of spring friendship.

Close with prayer and extinguish the candle.

Chapter 3

Spring Friendship

Being New Together

Bitter, but real,
Naomi was welcomed by Bethlehem.
Ruth ignored as a foreigner,
invisible, unnamed.

They couldn't live without eating,
so Ruth went to work
in the fields where God
gave them food for life.

From silence to speech
the women claimed "we"
as they mothered each other
under God's wings.

Both single and married women have to make space and time for talking about the intimate details of their lives with their friends if friendship is to thrive. They learn to trust each other for loyalty and support in a thousand small encounters. Spring, the season of "we," develops as two people learn to depend on each other for basic needs: safety, nurture, and language.

Safety

Although the covenant faith of the Israelites decreed welcome and protection for the stranger and sojourner, Naomi and Ruth challenged the conventional patterns of relationship by arriving together with no place to go, no family or clan to provide a home for them.

When the two widows arrived in Bethlehem, the mood of the village was joyful because the spring harvest was just beginning, and everyone could see that food would be plentiful. Like birds on a warm spring morning, the women chattered and exclaimed about Naomi's return, wanting to know about her life since she had left. In response, Naomi refused the crowd's rejoicing and called herself Mara, "because the Almighty has made my life very bitter"(1:20). Although she and Elimelech had departed from Bethlehem because of famine, she remembered having left "full" with a husband and two sons, and now she was returning "empty" because they were gone. In her mind Naomi had left at the peak of her womanly power, even though the land was barren. Now the land was full, and she was the barren one, a hollow vessel with no obvious way to be filled.

Naomi had roots in the community stemming from her marriage to Elimelech, but her participation would have to take a new form because she had been gone so long and was now in a very different season of her life. And while desert hospitality required a generous welcome for male strangers, that did not mean two indigent widows would be housed and fed indefinitely. Not only would Naomi and Ruth have to find a new form for their friendship within the traditional patterns of marriage and family, but also the community would have to change because of their arrival. In the beginning, Bethlehem offered Naomi and Ruth a safe place to be together, but nothing else that would encourage them to develop a mutually nurturing spring friendship.

Although Naomi and Ruth's arrival in Bethlehem signaled a shift in the external season of their friendship—from winter into spring—conditions were chilly and unpredictable. Whatever bonding had taken place between the older woman and the younger one while they traveled in the desert remained unspoken. They had not yet become a pair, a clearly defined "we" of spring friends. The village women could not name them as partners either, because custom in Bethlehem was limited to conventional dyads—married couples, mothers with children— amid auxiliary family groupings.

Naomi's bitterness matched Ruth's marginal status, and the two women seemed bound only by their need for safety. Since Ruth could not participate in this community through any children of her own, she remained an outsider. And from Naomi's description of herself as "bitter," we know that she, too, saw her value in this particular community solely on the basis of a mother's role, no matter how rich her living experiences had been. Both women were aliens to the cultural norms for women in Bethlehem.

Finding a safe place to share such ragged shards of hope for a fresh start is not easy for women today. We live in a culture that puts a premium on confidence and control, autonomy and self-sufficiency. When we share newborn parts of our lives with someone else, we may experience fear at the childlike vulnerability thus exposed. When someone responds with care and concern for the infant beginnings—which continue to occur all through adult life—then a spring friendship is born. Some women do that with a therapist or a spiritual director; others discover a special friend with whom they can share a growing edge.

According to Lillian Rubin in *Just Friends*, sharing intimate details is the experience that most feeds women's friendships. She suggests that women learn to relate as they did with their mothers, speaking from their feelings—what they saw, heard, supposed, or feared—in endless detail. The men Rubin interviewed seemed baffled by "all that talk," and Rubin concludes that their resentment comes from a deep longing for a Good Mother whose presence alone would be enough to warm and soothe. For women, safety means space and privacy for verbal sharing with lots of emotional content. For men, proximity seems to be comfort enough. That means women will usually go outside of marriage to find someone to talk with, while men turn to their wives.

Today, marriage and family tend to be a closed and pressured circle, and female friendships often have to take place around the edges. Modern life has filled our lives to the breaking point, and we have lost the social matrix of stable neighborhoods, social clubs, and weekly worship that once provided the natural ground for friendships. Work rarely provides space for the personal issues that feed a female friendship, and while we may able to call or use e-mail to nurture a friendship, finding unstructured time when new or nonverbal things can arise without pressure is difficult.

Allowing the attraction between two women to develop in our culture may also evoke criticism and suspicion from others. We have sexualized everything so heavily that it takes a fair amount of self-confidence to make choices for a friendship if others (particularly one's mate) feel excluded as a dyad develops. If we understand the role of a spring friendship, however, it may help us to make it a priority when it is necessary to protect a new part of ourselves coming to birth.

Though we may feel a frightening vulnerability in either part of the Child-Mother pattern, neither person is locked into one role or the other. Spring friends shift back and forth between the Child and Mother roles, providing safety and companionship for each other through some new stage of life. In that process, spring friends draw boundaries around their "we-ness" and define a way of being together that gives them a unique identity as a pair. Ellen Goodman and Pat O'Brien convey this idea in the title of their book on friendship, *I Know Just What You Mean*. As they ended a year of living and writing together as Nieman Fellows at Harvard, they agreed that empathy—the ability to see, *really* see, what someone else is going through—was the key ingredient for their friendship and those they interviewed.

That kind of empathy is something I experienced initially with my two sisters in different ways. Mimi and I are just eighteen months apart, and we shared a room until I was in high school. Although we did not always agree, we developed a kind of radar for each other's feelings that I have always looked for in a friend. And with my eight years' younger sister, Barbara, there is a physical knowing that may go back to the days when I held her and fed her as a baby. We have a similar body type and temperament, and when we cook together in her kitchen at Thanksgiving or Christmas, we move in a kind of dance, knowing exactly where the other will be. Being with my sisters gives me a sense of safety and being at home in the world, and this is something I look for in friendships now. I know I was drawn to Marianne when I first met her at the Faith@Work leadership event because she seemed to have that body-knowing (as a former nurse) and a strong intuitive sense of connection and understanding of my life story. It felt to me as if she could "really see" what was going on for me.

Nurture

When Naomi declared that she had returned to Bethlehem without family, she essentially denied Ruth's very presence. Yet Naomi seemed totally dependent upon Ruth's younger energy. If they were going to survive, Ruth needed to take on the mothering role and find some way to provide food and shelter for both of them.

Bereft of a male provider and protector, Ruth initiated the question of nurture for both of them: "Let me go to the fields," she told Naomi, "and pick up the leftover grain" (2:2). Although couched as a request, Ruth's intention was clear: She was ready to take whatever risks were necessary to ensure their survival. Hebrew law directed landowners not to reap their fields to the border or clean the fields after the harvest, so that the poor could find enough food to sustain life (Leviticus 19:10). Although Ruth knew that the men in the fields preyed on unprotected women, she hoped to "find favor" from someone who would be protective and kind to her.

Perhaps because she had already crossed the boundary of safety when she left Moab, Ruth was now able to choose leaving the safety of Bethlehem's village walls for the rough environment of the grain fields. She had already confronted her fears of physical violation and starvation when she committed herself to a relationship with Naomi (and with Naomi's God). Through a combination of trust and desperation, Ruth was ready to take her pledge to Naomi one step further and enter the harvest fields to find food, risking attack or violation for the sake of life itself. Ruth was already under the protective wing of Yahweh, but she had to live out her part of the dramatic story in order for God's provision to be seen. She became the catalyst for God's active care, not just the recipient.

Ruth's courage stirred Naomi out of wintry silence: "Go ahead, my daughter," she said (2:2). Naomi's use of the word "daughter" moved her back into a mothering role, proclaimed her willingness to make Ruth part of her family, and signified her readiness to link Ruth with the community, which the younger woman had already chosen. Naomi's blessing was the first sign of mutual commitment to the possibility of a spring friendship.

Even if Naomi could not join Ruth in the fields to help gather grain or provide some protection for her, she could claim a more active role in linking Ruth to the community. The biblical narrator provides a clue to that connection by prefacing Ruth's decision to work in the fields with the fact that "Naomi had a relative on her husband's side, from the clan of Elimelech, a man of standing, whose name was Boaz" (2:1). Thus Naomi carried the thread of clan connection for both of them, while Ruth's determination to work provided the link between Naomi's unclaimed family ties and their future together. They affirmed that there was life for women beyond marriage and motherhood, even in their patriarchal society.

In our day, spring friendships function in much the same way: as a dyad from which the energy for taking risk can come. While marriage or an old friendship can function as a primary unit of trust, encouragement for an emerging aspect of self will come from a friendship where growth can be extended beyond usual patterns. These spring partners can nourish our new growth because they are not invested in maintaining earlier life patterns.

Just as a baby requires food for life and growth, a spring friendship requires care and feeding. The biological role that women play in suckling children has been extended by our culture into nurturing the entire family—physically, emotionally, and spiritually. Women are often depleted by that role and must learn to recognize how they have denied their own needs for the sake of others. A female friendship, where neither partner is locked into being the nurturing Mother or the needy Child, may be a vital necessity for restoring the balance of give and take in our lives. Nurturing between women takes many forms, but it usually begins with the questions "What do you need?" followed by, "How can I help?"

What is needed is not always obvious. Often it is someone to listen without giving advice or trying to solve "a problem." In the beginning, commitment to a new friendship (or an old one in new circumstances) may be one-sided, as Ruth's was, but the direction may be set by the other's need, as with Naomi. This imbalance exists at the heart of any mother-child dyad, and it may be repeated in adulthood whenever one person experiences a crisis of new growth while another responds with care or concern. In a healthy spring friendship, that kind of mothering will be mutual over time.

When entering a new or hostile environment, we all need somebody who will say "Go for it!" The tone in which those words are said makes all the difference. A mother who is struggling with the fusion of childhood might, after a long argument, grudgingly say to a teenage daughter, "Go ahead," but a friend who stands in that mothering role may be able to freely bless a new endeavor without needing to control the outcome. As a commitment to caring about what happens, the words "Go for it!" characterize spring friendships that encourage growth and risk. The blessing and encouragement of those words literally feed our emerging self.

When I first met Marianne in 1977, we were both at a new stage of life. She was getting her doctorate in clinical psychology, and I was beginning to do retreat work using clay on a potter's wheel as an image of spiritual growth. The leadership training offered by Faith@Work gave us an extended period of common experience and an exciting conceptual framework of relational theology. Two consecutive weeks in a conference setting provided a special container to nurture our work in the world, separate from the daily demands of being at home. Although I initially took a mothering role with Marianne in her release of grief, when she got back to her home in Chicago, she took on the mothering role in our relationship. She encouraged some churches in the Chicago area to invite me to come with my potter's wheel, and she offered me a place to stay and transportation. She became my advocate and sponsor as I stepped into a more public role combining art and narrative theology.

Nurturing a spring friendship can take many forms, but physical care with housing, food, and transportation are simple and direct needs that we often overlook. When our energy is going into a new internal frontier, someone who will care about those physical details feels like a manifestation of The Great Mother. And when a friend can also care about the internal dynamics of newness, buds form into flowers and open to the warmth of new light.

Language

While safety and nurture are two important aspects of a spring friend-ship, a third vital aspect is finding language for what is happening—developing a story so the relationship can thrive over time. Nelle Morton, in her book *The Journey Is Home*, describes this as "hearing each other into speech." For women, that kind of listening is especially important because we often act from a feeling place but cannot explain it. Bringing images to speech provides a way of interpreting and under-standing what is coming into being. It is essential for consciousness. The combination of safety, nurture, and speech gives us a sense of belonging, of being "at home" in the world. As a mother helps a child develop lan-guage as a tool for moving away from her, dialogue with a spring friend helps us integrate newness and let go of old or outdated patterns of behavior.

Ruth's decision to enter the ripened fields of Bethlehem allowed her to participate directly in the abundance that Yahweh had provided for the Hebrews. Language for what was happening as she stepped into God's narrative through Israel would come. For now, Ruth's actions placed the interdependent bond between her and Naomi within the context of God's care and protection. As a field laborer, she left her dead past and stepped into the physical and spiritual bounty of the present.

"As it turned out," the biblical narrator states, Ruth "found herself" working in the fields of Boaz (2:3). When Boaz came to his field and noticed Ruth, he asked his foreman, "Whose young woman is that?" (2:5). The foreman described Ruth by the characteristic that was important to the people of Bethlehem: She was a foreigner who had come back with Naomi. He also made note of her hard-working dedication, saying, "[She] has worked steadily from morning till now except for a short rest in the shelter" (2:7).

Boaz was surprised to learn that Ruth belonged to no man. He was quick to offer her the protection she lacked, saying that she should stay with his crew of gleaning women, that he had directed the men "not to touch you," and further, that she could drink from the water they had drawn (2:9). Boaz gave her the safety and nurture in a public arena that Ruth's friendship with Naomi provided in the personal and private sphere.

Ruth's independence, courage, and lively curiosity were shown by her question to Boaz: "Why have I found such favor in your eyes that you notice me—a foreigner?" (2:10). She did not attribute the favor to God, but met Boaz face-to-face with her question. Her tone was direct, her self-confidence probably surprising to Boaz. She was probing for language to describe what was already taking place. She named her role as an outsider and forced him to verbalize his relationship to her. This was no coy flirtation, but the beginning of a dialogue that would provide language for her place in Bethlehem. Ruth asked a probing question that pushed beyond the boundaries of propriety and humble acceptance of Boaz' beneficence. She was no child of his, nor was she a humble servant or piece of property.

Boaz answered in terms of her sacrifice for Naomi, saying that Ruth's willingness to leave her homeland and come with Naomi had touched him. He also extended the discussion beyond his response to Ruth to the outer limits of his system of thought: "May the Lord repay you for what you have done. May you be richly rewarded by the Lord, the God of Israel, under whose wings you have come to take refuge" (2:12). His words gave Ruth an image for what was already happening: The God of Israel was like a mother hen providing protection for her chicks. Boaz expanded their dialogue from the immediate, literal question of Ruth's safety and nourishment to the world of spirit, of covenant promise, and God's Mothering presence around them all.

On the surface, Boaz' words tell us a good deal about him. He admired Ruth's commitment to Naomi. He was sensitive to what it meant to be a foreigner among the Hebrews. He was aware of Ruth's vulnerability in a strange land. In other words, he recognized her as a capable and responsible human being, not an object to be used and abused. According to the New Testament genealogy of Jesus, Boaz had a foreign mother himself: Rahab, the harlot in Jericho who saved Gideon and his men (Matthew 1:6). Whether or not that was historically accurate, listing Rahab as his mother—who would have been slaughtered by the invading Israelites except for her special role in helping to protect them—tells us something about the kind of experience that might have shaped Boaz with a different sensibility from others who would have treated Ruth with disdain. Boaz responded with kindness as Ruth claimed the refuge that he offered her.

After assuring Ruth of his protection, Boaz invited her to share food as well: "She ate all she wanted and had some left over" (2:14). Ruth took the excess home to Naomi, who recognized the sign of God's provision for both of them. "That man is our close relative," Naomi said, acknowledging Boaz' family ties with Elimelech (2:20). Naomi must have remembered the rumor that God had provided food for her people and recognized the generosity of Boaz as a sign to her from God.

The dialogue between Ruth and Boaz gave a new and larger context to what was happening around and through them. Ruth named the role that normally would have kept her outside of the community of Bethlehem and outside of the covenant: She was a particularly despised Moabite foreigner (Deuteronomy 23:3). And yet Ruth claimed her place with dignity and directness. Rather than begging for protection, Ruth asked Boaz to articulate the connection from his position inside the community norms that would have rejected her. Boaz answered respectfully, honoring Ruth's commitment to Naomi: "I have been told all about what you have done for your mother-in-law since the death of your husband—how you left your father and mother and your home-land and came to live with a people you did not know before" (2:11). Boaz saw her from a larger perspective, with God's eyes, instead of within the limitations of his culture. Their dialogue revealed his feeling for Ruth and his hope that God would reveal a way to include Ruth among the covenant people of Judah. Ruth clearly felt seen, known, respected, and loved.

We, too, can help each other interpret and understand events that might seem unrelated, accidental, or portentous. We can hear each other into speech, and love each other toward wholeness, with our questions and our caring. That is the soulwork of friendship. Finding words and images for our feelings or intuitions brings the power of understanding to our previously unnamed actions, and then we our-selves become living words to others. Spring friends engage in dialogue, as Boaz did with Ruth, naming what has not been understood before.

The presence of Boaz in Ruth's story raises another interesting question. Although most of my close friends have been women, there have been a few men, too. The one who most helped me find speech for the spiritual dimensions of my work as a potter was an Episcopal priest whom I met at an art show in 1971. I was there displaying my pots, and Michael was sitting with his wife's paintings for the day. Since there were few customers, we had lots of time to talk. Like Boaz, he responded openly and moved easily from particular observations to spiritual connections and images. He saw beyond the surface of my words and heard the undercurrents of my questions: He listened with his eyes. When Peter came to help me pack up my display, we went to their house and soon discovered friendship as two couples.

Within the safety of our foursome, Michael and I were able to nurture our mutual interest in dream images, poetry, and biblical stories, as well as to share the external world of meals and movies that we enjoyed as couples. Spring friendship developed as we discovered safety, nurture, and language for newborn parts of our lives. I was just beginning to explore the theological possibilities of clay and creativity, and we were both drawn to spiritual aspects of the physical world—the stories behind old tools and trunks, shellshapes, and falling stars in the night sky. This fed our spring friendship over the years.

When Michael took a parish farther south in Virginia Beach, he sent poems or book references to keep our connection alive. Infrequent family visits and periodic retreats that I led in his church provided us with times to nourish our spring friendship. He opened the world of Jungian dreamwork for Peter and me, and when he studied at the Jung Institute in Zurich in 1982, we drove from our place in Stuttgart, Germany, to visit and travel together. When I became president of Faith@Work in 1985, he was the only person inside "the church" who saw the fit between my gifts and this ecumenical ministry. I felt mothered by him in many ways, but he let me know that I was tending new growth in him as well. Then, in 1987, Michael was killed in a car accident. It was a terrific loss—for me and for many, many people—but by then I had internalized his belief in my call and ministry within Faith@Work.

We all need to be seen as Ruth was by Boaz, with empathy and care. Whether woman or man, when somebody notices with tenderness and affection who we are and what we are doing in the world, we can sense the new life within us because it is being mirrored back. Underneath Ruth's question "Why have you noticed me?" is the universal longing for recognition, encouragement, and understanding. And every time we are seen and named by those who love us, we are empowered to live more fully, more freely. A good mother does that from the very beginning, as her child is learning to walk and talk. When we grow up, we still need to hear those words of blessing for the stumbling and awkward parts of our lives. A spring friend, male or female, provides safety, nurture, and language for the new parts of ourselves that must be brought into consciousness throughout our lives. Those dyadic relationships shelter and sustain new growth until it can be integrated. Spring friendship is based on being new together.

For Personal Reflection

Safety

- Where do you find space and time for talking with a special friend?
- What qualities or conditions make you feel safe enough to risk a new beginning in yourself? In a friendship?
- Have you ever experienced an external threat or challenge that promoted internal bonding in a spring friendship? How did you and your friend create safety for each other?

Nurture

- How do you nurture a special friendship? Where do you go? What do you do?
- What is the role of food between you?
- Consider the ways in which your soul is "fed" by a spring friend.

Language

- In what part of your life do you feel wordless or awkward with language? Is there someone who "hears you into speech"? How does that happen?

For a Group

(15 minutes)

As your group meets for the third time, begin with the ritual of gathering that you have established. Spread a cloth or scarf for the altar and light the candle. Open with a prayer, a song, a chant, or a period of quieting silence. Then read the poem that begins this chapter. Invite each person to place her symbol of spring friendship on the altar cloth, saying a few words about why she chose this symbol.

(10 minutes)

Use the poem to review the main points of spring friendship from this chapter. Include the chapter's focus on the archetypal image of Mother and Child—and how those roles change back and forth in spring friendship.

(45 minutes)

Ask the group to form triads with people different from the previous session. Offer these questions for consideration:

- Is there someone who is, or has been, a spring friend for you?
- What is, or was, the new birth being called forth?
- How do you, or did you, hold your friend's newness as well?

(20 minutes)

Return to the whole circle. Invite each person to retrieve her symbol of spring friendship from the altar and name a learning about spring friendship from this session.

Ask the group to read chapter 4 for next week and bring with them a symbol of summer friendship.

Close with a quiet prayer and extinguish the candle.

Chapter 4

Summer Friendship
Searching for Call and Identity

"Is it not my duty," Naomi said,
"to see you settled?"
Hungry for place
and progeny she was.

Ruth listened
heard call
but did not see the path.
"I will do what you say . . . "

"Go wash and anoint yourself,"
Naomi counseled,
"then go to him by night,
and he will tell you what to do."

She went
to lie with Boaz
on the threshing floor,
her body a sacrament
for them both.

Boaz lay alone
with winter in his soul.
He didn't tell her what to do,
but asked instead,
"Who are you?"

"Will you redeem us?"

"I will," he whispered,
"but stay with me till dawn . . . "
"Why me?" he asked.
"You could have a younger man."

As light brushed the sky,
she left
full-filled with grain
and promise.

*S*ummer is the season of "I am," of independence, of pushing beyond friends who give us home and help to a new place where we can establish a separate identity. We feel hungry and thirsty for something more, or something different, because we have outgrown the cozy comfort of spring closeness, or because the wells of inner nourishment have dried up. We want purposeful work to do in the world or, at a deeper level, to understand our "call" from God. Differences become sharper as we separate "I" from "you," and we learn to put that distinction into words. Competition and envy can darken the sky of a summer friendship like a thunderstorm. Summer friends are usually individuals who travel alone on intersecting paths, sharing their hunger, rituals, and discovery.

Hunger

Differences between Naomi and Ruth increased as the spring barley harvest came to an end and summer began. Naomi was still hungry for a place to belong and for progeny to continue the family name among her people. She knew what it was to be literally homeless and starving, and it propelled her into action. She remembered the shift from bounty to famine years before when, as a young wife, she and Elimelech had fled their starving homeland in search of food. She was even more vulnerable this time as an older woman. She and Ruth had no "safety net" of family or friends, although Naomi could see possibilities for help from Boaz.

"My daughter," Naomi began, "should I not try to find a home for you, where you will be well provided for? Is not Boaz, with whose servant girls you have been, a kinsman of ours?" (3:1-2). To understand the daring plan that Naomi conceived, we need to know the Hebrew tradition of kinsman-redeemer. Naomi's people believed that God had given each of the twelve tribes a portion of the Promised Land in perpetuity. If one member was forced to sell his land, a wealthier kinsman could redeem it for the extended family. Further, in the tradition of levirate succession, a kinsman-redeemer might be expected to father a child with the widow to reestablish a man's line, although that was only law in the case of a dead brother's widow.[5]

Naomi saw a way to secure Ruth's future by asking Boaz to become their kinsman-redeemer, even though she knew there was a nearer relative who has first claim. Just when their human story seemed over and done with, God's call to new life stirred in Naomi, and she took the initiative. As Joan Chittister says in her book on Ruth, "To send Ruth to Boaz is to flaunt all the conventions of Israel. Except one: justice."[6]

While spring friends thrive in the present moment, summer friendships hold the tension of difference as their vision extends into the future. For Naomi and Ruth, it was a balance between sustaining a long-term vision for their future and meeting immediate physical needs. Differences in their ages and energy levels reinforced the cultural differences between them: Naomi knew the customs and laws of Bethlehem, while Ruth probably did not know what their options really were. Naomi was seeking a more permanent place in the community for both of them, while Ruth focused on the daily task of providing food. They each brought their separate strengths to the dilemma they shared. That this might be God's call or intention seems only to have occurred to Naomi, not Ruth. Naomi was willing to trust God's provision because she could read the signs of God's presence in the way Ruth had been seen with such respect by Boaz.

Hunger for change is often the seedbed for call, an inner drive toward identity and expression in the world, which is also a mark of our full humanity. Summer friends encourage that in one another. On the surface, it seems that our culture expects women to be "happily settled" in marriage and, by implication, fulfilled and not ambitious for a separate identity. But most women today recognize a deeper call to life that is a combination of being at home with ourselves and doing something in the world, something that is a unique expression of "I am." For some, this call may be expressed through parenting, but there are many other ways for women to experience God's call to life. The search for our call to BE ALIVE emerges in the restlessness of our summer souls—probing, risking, and reaching beyond what we know and have. When we share that hungering and thirsting with someone who is also reaching beyond her present situation, we find a summer friend to walk with.

In summer friendships, differences are more apparent than common cause. Age, temperament, and experience point to otherness and detachment rather than the soul-friend compatibility of springtime. Competition can arise if two friends work in the same field or want the same kind of recognition. Old feelings of rivalry (and inadequacy) left over from high school may surface in new forms. Over time, other differences begin to show up. One friend values planning and promptness; the other is more spontaneous. One heads back to school for more preparation, another seeks a new work situation where more opportunities for challenge and advancement are available. The time for testing our skills and stretching our capabilities may eventually take us in different directions, but during the summer period, differences between friends stimulate growth and stretch us beyond our comfort zone, though the relationship may strain in the charged atmosphere of challenge, competition, and call.

As a season of separateness and individuality, summer seems antithetical to lasting friendships. Yet for Ellen Goodman and Pat O'Brien, newspaper writers who wrote about their long-term friendship in *I Know Just What You Mean,* outward differences soon gave way to a deeper soul connection between their more vulnerable but fuller selves:

> Pat saw a confident, breezy insider, but she couldn't see the missteps or wrenching changes. Ellen saw Pat's conventional surface, but not the rebellious soul, and certainly not the pulls of tradition and independence that had defined so much of her adult life and that would be a running dialogue of our twenty-six-year conversation.[7]

The contrasting pulls of tradition and independence that Goodman and O'Brien identify run through many long-term friendships, particularly in the summer season. Externally, Marianne and I found work in separate spheres. Mine was more public and communal, leading retreats for Faith@Work and speaking at different denominational gatherings. Her work was intimate and intense, working one-to-one with psychotherapy clients, lives seemed to be going in different directions, but underneath there was a deep connection expressed by home, family, and faith that we also shared. Although our hungers for impact and recognition were different, some kind of spiritual integrity held us together. Maybe the physical distance between us helped to absorb some of the competition we might have felt if we were living in the same community. During the years when work took us in such different directions, with very different schedules, I wondered if our friendship would survive.

Ritual

In their summer friendship Naomi took the part of a priest or wisdom figure, telling Ruth exactly how to proceed. She had a sense of what Ruth needed to do in order to succeed in getting Boaz to bypass a nearer relative. "Wash and perfume yourself," she said, "and put on your best clothes. Then go down to the threshing floor, but don't let him know you are there until he has finished eating and drinking." The plan was simple and dangerous: After her preparation, Ruth would go to the threshing floor under cover of darkness, find Boaz among the other men, lie down with him, and then follow his directions. We are left to imagine the rest.

"I will do whatever you say," Ruth answered Naomi. At this point in the story, Ruth became the obedient initiate, committing herself to Naomi's plan without considering any other options. Ruth's preparation included more than just making herself as attractive as possible; her cleansing ritual had religious overtones as well. This was to be a sacred journey, a ritual descent into darkness and danger. She would have to pass among the very field hands who had posed a threat to her safety when she had first gone to work in the fields; she would become "fair game" for any of them who awoke to find her on the threshing floor at night. Then she would have to approach the man who had power to destroy or redeem her life. Ruth would undertake a classical heroic journey as she walked the path between death and redemption on her way toward Boaz.

Ruth's ritual preparation symbolically connected the inner and outer dimensions of this important transition. When Ruth washed her body, she was not only cleansing her skin, but washing away her fears as well. When she anointed her body, she was softening her skin with oil and perfume, but the word "anointed" also connotes the holy work she was doing. Ruth's preparation was a sign of her own baptism, her trust that this journey lay in God's hand.

Although we live in a material culture where "what you see is what you get," most of us sense a spiritual reality pervading the physical, and ritual is one way of connecting with that intangible realm of spirit. Churches used to provide sacred rituals for the important transitions of birth, marriage, and death, but reverence for the divine dimension of human experience has largely drained away in our culture of secular individualism. We often find ourselves adrift without meaningful rituals for soulful shifts. Instead, we have ritual contests, such as the Olympics or NBA basketball, or elaborate wedding parties, in an effort to provide a substitute for the hungers that our souls have for living symbols that mediate the unconscious.

In popular culture we understand the practice of focusing our energies with ritual behavior: Athletes go through a specific routine before an important contest; musicians prepare for a concert in practiced ways; even computer programmers develop certain patterns to unknot a problem. But the question of finding someone who understands the spiritual dimension of a larger shift is more difficult because, for the most part, our culture has lost an understanding of sacred initiation.

Creating ritual outside the church became more common in the late seventies, when women began to claim that "what's personal is political," and we became conscious of how institutional structures ignored sexual abuse and the physical trauma that marked the lives of so many women. Around the country women began to form ritual groups to celebrate many different aspects of their lives that had been neglected by formal religious practices: changing seasons in nature, personal transitions, family and community junctures. Just as Ruth washed and anointed herself for her sacred journey to the threshing floor, women gathered in local groups, formal and informal, to acknowledge trials and celebrate the seasons of our lives. We recognized that rituals of recollection and remembering are important aspects of preparing ourselves for risk and change, and we discovered that we could move beyond institutional forms that did not feed us.

As spiritual hunger turns to intention, preparation becomes essential, and we need those with a larger view to help us understand the archetypal spiritual dimension of internal change as it arrives. Often a therapist serves as a summer companion or guide, but because of professional boundaries, cannot actually be a summer friend. Because a shift in our sense of identity, or a response to a new "call," may require intense study or complete withdrawal, we may need a summer friend who will assist and support—or at least understand the need for—ritual preparation. A summer friend is one who sees the need for ritual, one who will focus on conscious choices: the "I am, I can, I will" of self.

When Marianne and I realized that we both wanted more ritual for important passages in our lives than the church could provide, we discovered that we could create our own. Our shared Protestant Christian tradition gave us symbols to work with. Her studies gave me language. My art fed her images. When Marianne and I shared the steps she took in getting a birth certificate for the child they had lost, I was able to let her grief work lead me into the unknown territory of my own infertility. Our first ritual was a memorial service for their long-dead child. I made an urn for Danny's burial and, during that time, I also made a large coiled pot shaped like a papoose that stood in my pottery studio as a "guardian angel" for the children Peter and I never had.

Another ritual that gave our friendship a richer field was family visits. Spending time with her immediate family happened naturally when I came to Chicago for speaking engagements, but the first time I came with no other purpose than to attend her graduation, her grown sons kept probing for the reason. "Just to celebrate," I said, "because I'm really proud of your mom." Marianne's visit to Bellingham, Washington, to see the land where I had grown up, and to meet my parents while Peter was on an assignment in Germany, was even more of a special event. It gave us direct experience with the personalities and peculiarities of family that let us claim the similarities of immigrant background and the differences of education and energy that shaped us. It would be ten more years before a book came into my hand that spoke to the need for women's ritual to honor such passages. Judith Duerk's *Circle of Stones* has touched many lives with her invitation:

> How might your life have been different if there had been a place for you, a place for you to go to be with your mother, with your sisters and the aunts . . . a place of women to go, to be, to return to, as woman? How might your life be different?[8]

She describes a circle of women who would welcome our feelings of sadness and tears, welcome our body changes, provide a monthly retreat during menstruation, help with childbirth, and honor lives lost through miscarriage or abortion. When I read Judith's book, I felt my deep gratitude for walking with Marianne through those turbulent years when each of us was establishing our separate career paths.

Discovery

Summer friends recognize their differences and operate independently. Like polar opposites in a magnetic field, summer friends are related by common interests or common goals, but they may repel each other when forced together. Each must feel free to choose their times of intimacy and vulnerability. Because of their essential separateness, discovery of a deeper current between summer friends may come as a surprise or even a shock of spiritual connection.

When Ruth decided to approach Boaz at night on the threshing floor, she claimed her own power to risk life and death. Naomi could not do it for her. Although Ruth had undertaken a similar journey by day when she went to the barley fields, she was entering a more highly-charged field this time. Even though darkness gave her some protection, she would not be able to see Boaz and might approach the wrong man. And if she found Boaz, he might not agree to do what she asked; he might not be willing to interrupt village customs in order to redeem the two women.

Following the meal that Boaz shared with the other harvesters, Ruth noticed where he lay down. When it was dark, she went to him, uncovered his feet, and lay down as Naomi had directed. Whether uncovering his feet was a biblical euphemism for nakedness or sexual intercourse, or simply an act that would cause him to stir in his sleep to find a warm covering again, uncovering his feet signified Ruth's active invitation to intimacy.

According to Naomi's direction, Boaz would tell Ruth what to do when he awakened. All she had to do was begin their interaction. But when Boaz woke in the night to find a woman lying with him, he did not tell her what to do. Instead he asked, "Who are you?" Suddenly Ruth was in the position of accepting her power and presence there. She was not simply an agent of Naomi's scheme nor a lonely woman looking for comfort after too much wine. She had prepared herself in a ritual way for this engagement. She had come to ask for help, to seek a path of survival for herself and Naomi. As she had in making her vow to Naomi, Ruth once again chose into God's story by her own volition.

"I am your servant Ruth," she answered with her own name. "Spread the corner of your garment over me, since you are a kinsman-redeemer" (3:9). Answering with her own name and presenting a clear, straightforward request defined her separate identity. She told Boaz what to do, not the other way around. She took the initiative to get the intervention that she and Naomi needed. It would be easy to see this as an economic exchange—of trading sexual favors for social gain—but then we would miss the sacred drama entirely. As he spread his cloak over them both, he enacted the very blessing he spoke when they met: He gave her refuge beneath the wings of Yahweh (2:12).

When Ruth called Boaz a "kinsman-redeemer," she identified a role for him that still belonged to the future. It would require his cooperation and a favorable judgment by the city elders. The purpose of redemption among the Hebrews was to secure the property of a family and provide a male heir. And since conception was thought to be a gift of God, by inviting Boaz to conceive a child with her, Ruth was not only claiming the right to provide a male heir for Naomi but was claiming the power of Naomi's God as well. Against the backdrop of her childless marriage to Naomi's son Mahlon, Ruth's whispered invitation to Boaz was also a confession of faith!

In response to Ruth's words, Boaz revealed his own vulnerability: "May Yahweh bless you, my daughter," the aging man replied, "for this last act of kindness of yours is greater than the first, since you have not gone after young men, poor or rich" (3:10 JB). His blessing echoed Naomi's blessing; the two older figures—man and woman—acknowledged Ruth's identity and call. Ruth's honesty evoked his own. Her invitation brought him hope. Boaz came down off his pedestal of authority and control, and with his words, "Bless you, my daughter," he let Ruth know that they were mutually involved in redeeming life for each other. They each discovered another part of themselves in their relationship.

Boaz concluded this part of the story by committing himself to do what Ruth asked of him. "Have no fear then," Boaz said, "I will do whatever you ask, for the people of Bethlehem all know your worth" (3:12 JB). With these words, Boaz made an unconditional commitment to be guided by Ruth. From his stance within the community, he guessed that he would succeed in his effort to redeem Ruth and Naomi, but his response also suggests that he was sensitive to the chance Ruth had taken. Perhaps he remembered Rahab, his foremother, in a similar nighttime encounter and wanted to reassure Ruth that her safety and her future were important to him.

Boaz responded to Ruth's initiative from his position within the cultural system of Bethlehem. He protected Ruth by rousing her "before the hour when one man can recognize another, for," he said, "it must not be known that this woman came to the threshing floor" (3:14 JB). He was aware that Ruth could have been molested or stoned if the other men discovered her there. He also recognized the danger of community censure because their nighttime liaison was beyond the limits of cultural approval. Protecting her reputation with the towns-people was important to the negotiations that lay ahead of him because his success in redeeming them depended upon recognizing the social forces around them.

As Ruth prepared to leave the threshing floor, Boaz filled her cloak with six measures of barley as a sign to Naomi that he would be their kinsman-redeemer. It was a sign of his promise, a fulfillment of his pledge even before the deed was done. Moreover, the grain was a potent symbol of God's abundance and blessing on their union.

When Ruth returned, Naomi recognized the depth of his commit-ment, saying, "Wait . . . and see how things will go, for he will not rest until it is settled" (3:18 JB). Though Ruth and Boaz were the principal actors in this scene of the story, Naomi began and ended their encounter with her words. She was the prophetic voice, interpreting events from God's larger perspective. Each of them had a unique role to play in this sacred drama. Each brought different needs to the spectrum of their relationship: maturity and aging, woman and man, poverty and wealth. As they honored their differences, God's larger story took form and substance through them, and they discovered how to say "yes" to the possibilities for new life. It was Naomi who named the sacred dimension of their interaction. She was the celebrant and priest for their ritual union. But it was Boaz' question "Who are you?" that cata-pulted Ruth into the discovery of her call and identity.

As women, we are still encouraged to find an identity as somebody's daughter, wife, or mother. Just because feminism has brought us new awareness of our individuality does not mean that we have done the inner work to free ourselves from being unconsciously bound by those relationships. In spite of many freedoms, women are still socialized *not* to ask, "Who am I?" In her book *Just Friends,* Lillian Rubin describes the role of friendship as calling forth our individuality, our uniqueness, helping us name our separateness. Summer friends are those who will persist with the probing question "Who are you?" and travel the road of discovery with us.

Discovery is the result of dialogue, of unfolding revelation, of bringing our experience to the encounter for examination, evaluation, and understanding of how it relates to our sense of self. When someone asks us who we are, the name we give carries an echo of character, of soul. Understanding our sexuality is one part of establishing our identity as a woman in the world. Another piece is to understand how our sexual nature is perceived by others, particularly by the men around us. That means we especially need a summer friend at those critical times when our bodies change, when mothering or its equivalent has been completed. A summer friend is someone who has Naomi's long-term vision and is willing to live with the largeness of our life purpose questions— and the answers as they arrive.

We discover who we are when we walk in the charged, dark fields of harvest, hunting for God's "yes" partially hidden among the sleeping bodies. The image of Boaz and Ruth lying together on the threshing floor also raises the issue of touch, intimacy, and sexuality in our friendships. Sharing new aspects of self, whether inward or outward, can generate strong feelings of attraction that our society quickly labels "sexual." Our faith tradition recognizes the force of "agape love" as Jesus practiced it—although it is clear from recent scandals that humans do not always draw appropriate boundaries.

Jungians have helped us understand the process of projecting both our gifts and our "demons" out onto other people as something new is coming into consciousness. John Sanford, who was both an Episcopal priest and a Jungian therapist, described this clearly in his book *The Invisible Partners*: Often we "fall in love" with a part of ourselves that we can see in another. A summer friend is someone who can help us sort that out. As Marion Woodman says in her tape series, *Conscious Aging*, "Desire is the engine of internal change." Acting on that attraction can, and does, stop the inner growth process by making the attraction concrete and literal, binding us to another at a physical level rather than letting the "heat" of passion be a transmuting fire. A summer friend can help us name and know the difference between sexual attraction and spiritual passion.

Without personal consciousness, or the conservative safeguards of a community context, sexual attraction can, and does, release explosive energy which, in turn, can destroy old patterns of loyalty. A "midlife crisis" can become a trap instead of an invitation to consciousness. Many women's friendships are quickened by the girlish secrets of feeling the power rising in our bodies with a new sense of "who I am" in the world and discovering other ways to express it than by hopping into bed with a man. Acknowledging sexual energy and channeling it toward the functional goals of a summer friendship brings an edge to this season that will be missing in other seasons.

With Marianne, I was able to talk about a keener sense of "who I am" in the world without feeling disloyal to my husband. As we looked for ways to feed our friendship and find time to be together without other responsibilities, she and I went off to a women's wilderness intensive in the boundary waters near Ely, Minnesota, with about twenty other therapists. Nervous and self-conscious at first, I began to realize that we each came with the same question: "Who am I *now?*" (rather than "Who have I *been?*") and "Who am I *becoming?*"

In the mornings and evenings, we worked hard in a therapeutic environment. In the afternoons, we swam and sunbathed nude, displaying the scars of births and deaths on our bodies in the safe circle of women there. I felt a sense of body-soul connection that I remembered from childhood. I came away knowing that my body is truly sacred, part of God's divine creation, and not simply a container. It was the first step in reclaiming the power of my woman's body for my work in the world, and I wouldn't have done it without Marianne's initiative.

Summer friends bring diversity, energy, and occasionally clashing interests to their relationship. A summer friend is one who respects the boundaries of individuality, welcomes differences as creative potential, and is protective of the other's dignity. A summer friend will help pose the questions "Who are you?" and "Who are you becoming?" without trying to determine the answer. In the tradition of Naomi, a summer friend will also recognize the signs of God's presence in our human affairs, and point to the holy, the sacred, and the archetypal elements in our earthy efforts.

For Personal Reflection

Hunger

- In the recent past, has there been a time of restless search that took you in a new direction? What were you hungry for?
- Was there a friend who took the role of Naomi for you? Or a friend like Ruth, for whom you saw a larger picture? If not, did you find that function somewhere else (With a therapist? A spiritual director? A mentor? A relative?) How did your hungers draw you together?

Ritual

- Identify a turning point in your recent past and describe a summer friend who helped you prepare for it. What did your friend say or do?
- Can you identify or imagine a preparation ritual for this turning point?
- When have you met a summer friend by entering a new or frightening situation? What did you discover about yourself in that encounter?

Discovery

- When has someone taken a risk on your behalf? What was "redemptive" about his or her action?
- Do you have a symbol or token from that event? What is it and how would you describe its symbolism?
- When have you felt sheltered or protected by a summer friend? What were the circumstances?

For a Group

(15 minutes)

Call the circle together. Prepare an altar, light a candle, and begin with a prayer, song, chant, or silence.

Then read the poem at the beginning of this chapter.

Invite each person to add her symbol of summer friendship to the altar, saying a brief word about why she chose this symbol.

(10 minutes)

Use the poem to focus the discussion on the question "Who are you?" Encourage participants to think about the inward and outward dimensions of identity.

(45 minutes)

Ask the group to form triads with people different from the previous session. Offer these questions for consideration:

- What is your experience of separateness, envy or competition, and difference in a summer friendship?
- What are the difficulties that a summer friendship might create for you? With a primary partner? Or among old friends?

(20 minutes)

As the group comes back to the whole circle, ask each person to retrieve her symbol from the altar and name a learning about summer friendship from this session.

Ask the group to read chapter 5 for next week and bring with them a symbol of community for autumn friendship.

Close with prayer and extinguish the candle.

Chapter 5

Autumn Friendship
Community Context

From summer singularity
to an autumn web of "us,"
Boaz came
to bargain for them
before the elders.

The kinsman with
a prior claim
said "yes" to land
but "no" to Ruth
to keep his land-line pure.

Then Boaz made his move
and so his name joined Ruth's
in David's line—
and Jesus's too—
the sandal as a sign.

The women wove their blessing
from scarlet threads
of Mother lore
that came before
Exodus and the Promised Land:
. . . Rachel and Leah,
one loved,
the other rich with many sons;
. . . Tamar, tricking Judah
into giving her an heir;
the women
welcomed Ruth
as one of us.

*a*utumn is the season of "us," where friendships are embedded in family and community with many surrounding relationships. What is singular and special in summertime becomes plural and tangled with many threads in the autumn season of friendship. Groups absorb the energy and diffuse the direction of summer friends, integrating individuality with traditions and customs. Community provides a field of other options and obligations in which friendship can either grow or wither. Rules, intercession, and confirmation mark the shift from summer to autumn.

Rules

Recognizing the power structure and unspoken rules of a community is the first step of entry. Naomi's visionary plan to bring Ruth into the social fabric of Bethlehem was expansive, inclusive, and full of autumn abundance, even though the social rules would have kept her out. Naomi never doubted the necessity of these traditions and taboos for them; nobody in the ancient world would have. Naomi was their primary link to community, and her initiative shifted their friendship from summer separateness to a more interactive phase as they moved toward a place in the village community. Naomi lived in trust that God would bless her stubbornness and welcome Ruth, though alien, to the fold.

When this story became part of the Jewish tradition after the Exile—when the move to purge Israel of foreign wives was at its peak—priestly rules would have denied Ruth a place in the social order, but God's provision was wider than that. The story has a subversive purpose, telling of God's welcome to a foreign woman in this deceptively simple love story.

In Bethlehem, where lines of inheritance determined who would get land to live on, Naomi knew she would need the help of a man because custom dictated male ownership of land. Women had no legal rights, though Hebrew law required community provision for widows and orphans. Naomi must have been reassured that God was guiding their path when Ruth returned with grain as a sign of Boaz' willingness to help them. Though Naomi did not have the power to accomplish her vision alone, or only with the help of Ruth, she had set into motion the forces that would eventually make them part of the community.

Boaz was the gateway to community for both women. He agreed to intercede for them with the village elders who met at the city gate to decide on local matters of property claims and inheritance. Like the mouth of a communal body, the gate was a place where the flow of commerce in goods and people could be managed and directed, sorting who should be admitted and who should be kept out. Rules and roles, power and tradition crossed at the village gate. The men who would make a decision about Boaz and Ruth probably squatted informally in a circle near the gate where they could watch the traffic and trade, exchange gossip, and make whatever rulings were needed to safeguard the orderly patterns of life in the village. Because they could make legally binding judgments, they had the power to release a closer relative in Elimelech's family from the option of redeeming Naomi and Ruth.

Naomi knew that Boaz understood the male power structure and how to maneuver within the tradition of kinsman-redeemer. When he first noticed Ruth, he had asked, "Whose woman is that?" Then he had been careful to send Ruth back from the threshing floor before dawn so she would not be seen and to preserve her reputation in the village. Boaz spoke as one with control over the lives of others, a landowner with money and property, a thinking man of the village who demonstrated his kindness by offering protection for Ruth. Perhaps Naomi chose Boaz over the nearer kinsman because she saw in Boaz someone who could be both a bridge between, and a gateway to, the community for them.

Ruth could not traverse community boundaries alone, and she could not make "your people" into "my people" by herself. Ruth's individual work had been effective in the fields where her labor and industry could be seen and appreciated. But when the harvest ended, Boaz could not "spread his wings over her" without drawing her inside the legal system of the community, where laws and customs would protect her when his personal power was not enough. Naomi's vision and Boaz' action were both essential in order for the two women to enter the covenantal fabric of Bethlehem.

Today, the problem is not so much *getting* into a community as *finding* one. We try to make a marriage with children into community enough because we think there is no time or place for more, but then we lose touch with the complex mystery of what it means to deal with people who are truly different from ourselves. At work, we may hope to find community in association and common tasks, but increasingly people are treated as interchangeable parts, hired or replaced as profit margins dictate. When making a profit is the basic motivation, we do not experience the mutual accountability of a creative social organism. Common leisure activities may give the appearance of community, because people do the same thing at the same time in the same place with the same rules, but mutual commitment to act together on behalf of the whole is usually missing from a leisure bond. Where to find a sacred container with common stories, traditions, and rituals is a question for most of us. We cram friendships into the scarce moments around the edges of our busy schedules and have largely stopped looking for intentional community because we imagine it would take too much time and effort.

In reality, we have the same amount of time that humans have always had, but our priorities are different. In our consumer society, we have put money and things ahead of time for relationships. Technology separates us even as it promises more ways to be "in touch." In our nomadic culture we increasingly live in isolation, naming the place where we live "our community," even though we do not know our neighbors and could not name the cohesive characteristics that define a true community. As a result, friendships may founder when family or work responsibilities take priority. Because the unconscious community of living in a small town is not the norm for most of us, we need to look for places where friendship is valued and acknowledged, where community is intentional. This could be an extended family grouping, a neighborhood action group or church, a sorority, or service club. Community comes in many forms.

Churches still provide one possibility for sacred community, but people need to do more than come every Sunday and sit in straight rows in order to make that potential into a functional reality. And if, like village walls, there are dogmatic boundaries that define a church community with a certain orthodoxy, then someone must have Naomi's larger vision to trust that God can, and will, open doors that humans have locked against strangers. Too often community means a tight tradition of unspoken norms, and there is no room for "the other," for a Ruth.

How we treat those at the margins may be the measure of a true spiritual community. It is easy to "dumb down" our differences and find the lowest common denominator as a mark of community, excluding others for the sake of our own version of a walled city. It is harder to find a community with permeable boundaries, a community that is clear about defining members and equally committed to caring for those who do not fit. Sometimes an extended family can manage to do that when they come together for celebratory occasions, such as a wedding or funeral. Churches have a biblical mandate to welcome "the stranger" and care for those at the economic and social margins, but even that does not guarantee a lively community will be found there.

Many of us never experience autumn friendships because we do not have the community context suggested by that season. Instead, we isolate a spring friendship at home and perhaps develop a summer friendship or two at work. But without a community to expand and develop those friendships, our relationships sour or become boring and then, in desperation, we move, shift jobs, or trade one partner for another. The full cycle of seasonal friendships simply does not develop.

For me, the community where I find my autumn friends is The Seekers Church, one of the sister communities that grew out of Church of the Saviour (CoS) in Washington, D.C. When Peter and I came back to Seekers after he retired from the army in 1982, I knew the time had come for me to claim my call to ministry, even though I did not know what form it would take. Peter was also open to guidance and direction in his choice of new work, and we were both looking for an autumn community where our friendships from other seasons could be integrated more fully. By then we had been married more than twenty years and were ready to settle down and invest ourselves in those relationships.

When we returned to Seekers, finding a gateway person was not difficult. Sonya had been one of the two founders, and she reached out as soon as we arrived. She usually initiated the contact, calling to get together over lunch or some other mutual interest. Mostly it was an occasion to talk . . . about everything. She seemed to enjoy my company and respect my observations. We socialized with Sonya and her husband on special occasions, such as anniversaries and birthdays. I felt included because she had a visible role and was making an effort to involve me as a person, not just somebody to do a job.

Sonya knew the unspoken rules of the Seekers community because she had been there from the beginning and had helped to shape The Seekers Church out of For Love of Children (FLOC). She had been drawn to FLOC, a separately incorporated mission of Church of the Saviour, while still a member of a suburban Virginia church. When Gordon Cosby, founder of CoS, urged the core missions of the church to become separate worshiping congregations in 1976, Sonya and Fred Taylor (director of FLOC) issued a call for Seekers to become a church where people could experience the call of God in the structures of daily life and work. Peter and I arrived just as this reformation was happening, and we were drawn to Seekers because of its vitality and commitment to lay leadership. I was also drawn by Sonya's presence in worship as the regular liturgist to balance the male preacher; it gave me a whole image of God, male and female, at the altar.

As with any established community, there are customs that structure village life at Seekers. Every member is expected to be asking, "What is God's call for me?" (the journey inward) and "Where am I called to serve others?" (the journey outward). Community life is the third dimension, nurtured by weekly mission groups and common worship. Seekers has no clergy staff. A different person from the community preaches every week, and the teaching function is accomplished through classes offered by members in the Tuesday night School of Christian Living. At Seekers, it is all crew and no passengers.

By the time I became president of Faith@Work, Seekers had confirmed my call to "outreach teaching" and given me a spiritual director who could be a companion for my inner growth, even though much of my work took place in other locations doing weekend retreats. For Peter, there was a separate and equally important path, through another mission group, to worship leadership and then a part-time staff position at Seekers. We have been challenged by the teachings of Jesus and the lives of other Seekers toward simplicity and generosity in matters of money and lifestyle. As part of a small church with a high degree of commitment and creativity from all members, we have both felt grounded and guided for the past thirty years there.

Intercession

Engaging the power and authority structures of the village is the second step of entering a community. Roles based on social and economic custom are critical to the community and speak of the values that hold a community together over time. And if our entrance to a community depends on challenging or changing those roles, we especially need an intercessor, someone in the community who can speak on our behalf.

Boaz was prepared to speak up for Naomi and Ruth. When the first claimant (who remained unnamed throughout this encounter) appeared at the gate, Boaz invited him to sit down with the elders. Boaz then introduced a new piece of information: He revealed that Naomi wanted to sell a piece of land that had belonged to Elimelech. Since married women did not normally participate in property ownership among the Jews, Naomi may not have known, when she first arrived in Bethlehem, that she had something to sell, but Boaz knew about the land. When he spoke, Naomi suddenly had worth and value in the city economy. Since land was regarded as a sacred gift from God, this transaction further revealed God's presence in the women's destiny.

Although Boaz offered Naomi's land to the first kinsman, Boaz made a clear statement of his intention to redeem the land if the man did not want to buy it from Naomi. However, the next of kin agreed to buy Naomi's field—perhaps expecting a bargain from the poor widow who had been absent from Bethlehem most of her adult life. But then Boaz added another crucial bit of information: "On the day you purchase the land from Naomi, you purchase Ruth the Moabitess also . . . and so restore [Elimelech's] name to his inheritance" (4:5 JB).

Upon hearing of Ruth's inclusion in the deal, the man retracted his claim. He did not want to jeopardize his own line of inheritance by the possibility of another claimant to his wealth, should Ruth conceive and bear a son. No mention was made of Ruth's ten-year marriage, or lack of conception, with Mahlon; the men simply assumed that Ruth would bear a child and so restore the family to its place in the community. There was no wonder, no mystery, no questioning of God's hand in their deliberations. On the surface, it was an economic question based on property ownership, resource control, and inheritance.

The transaction was completed when the first claimant removed his sandal and gave it to Boaz. The leather sandal, marked with this man's footprint, was a sign that would stand as evidence before tribal judges if there were any questions about the agreement with Boaz. From being just a simple shield for the wearer's feet, the sandal became a sign of relinquishment by the first man and a marriage promise by Boaz, blessed by the minion of elders. When the elders acknowledged the transaction, they recognized the property relationship between Naomi and Ruth, and approved the place that the women would both have as part of Boaz' household.

As a symbol for the unseen reality of God's part in the matrix of community, the sandal is a powerful metaphor that holds the dust of the earth along with the sweat and toil of its wearer. It speaks of the ground of our being, our humble connection with all living things that walk upon this earth, and the marvel of our uniqueness. Even today, a baby is recognized by its footprint on a birth certificate—the whorls and outline a unique signature of human life. In this story, the sandal is a symbol of one man's relinquishment and a sign of God's promise for Boaz.

The presence of God conveyed by the story of Ruth and Naomi is complex and communal, not exclusive or judgmental. Boaz welcomed this comely stranger when the nearer kinsman could not get beyond his property concerns, an elegant parallel to Orpah and Ruth's decisions in the first part of the story. In both examples, one person turns away from the invitation to God's creative complexity and diversity, and another person finds the courage to say "yes." When Orpah turned back, the story moved forward in Ruth's hands. When the kinsman turned away, Boaz offered the hope of new life.

Today, we may live through many physical seasons with only spring or summer friends to accompany us, while our souls yearn for an autumn spiritual community to validate the urge for relationship that is at the core of deep friendship. In our culture, we have so much suspicion of traditional roles and authority structures that we are likely to avoid association with people of different ages. Although some will find entrance to an autumn community an easy, natural process that develops from the ripening fruits of each season, most of us avoid community for fear that our summer individuality will be engulfed by autumn conviviality.

Fortunately, a longing for connection may draw us homeward again, whether to a physical place (as Naomi did) or to a new spiritual home (as Ruth found). In either case, we need to find a redeemer from within the community to act as an intercessor, someone who understands the inner structure of whatever community we are drawn to. We also need to be aware that, where there is simply a collection of individuals engaged in a common task, it is each one for herself or himself. The role of "redeemer" is possible only where genuine community exists.

Because we live in a materialist culture shaped by dualism that values thought over feeling, head over heart, we may start out like the unnamed "first claimant": more concerned about maintaining control, purity, and perfection than we are with welcoming the untamed and unknown parts of our selves. The path toward a chosen community may be partially blocked by family members who are like the nearest kinsman, having a "first claim" on our lives. Our parents provide the first image of community with set roles and responsibilities, and that shapes what we think we want, or want to avoid, in a chosen community. We often carry our childhood image of what a community is—colored by our feelings about parents and home—into adulthood. Then, like Ruth, we leave home, land, family, or other inheritance—and often a child-hood image of God as well. We may wander in the desert for a long time before we discover a matrix of autumn friends with whom we can redis-cover our own complexity in community.

Many women expect family to provide enough community for adult life, but usually that is too role bound for the fullness of who we are. Marriage begins as a spring friendship, where it can provide safety, nur-ture, and language. A marriage may survive the summer periods of stretching and growth, but it takes an autumn community of diverse friends to hold the changes that we will grow through. Without an autumn community, we do not have others with more experience to guide us into the deeper waters of our spiritual lives, to help us learn from those difficulties rather than flee with a fantasy of perfection somewhere else. Sometimes a crisis will break open the roles we have been playing with each other in marriage, but more often (according to statistics) we leave a marriage in a mistaken search outside ourselves for the truth of who we are and what we are here for.

Like Naomi, we can learn to live with a long view and trust our intu-ition about finding the way home again. And like Ruth, we may risk our very lives to find those companions who will be our redeemers along the way. Money and power are no substitute for the inner experience of self-discovery, but needing money can put us in situations that will call forth something deeper, more real and vital than we knew before. Necessity can be an invitation to examine what we are spending our life energy for, and how much is enough, in the light of what our planet can sustain. In the end, dealing with the power of money can be an invitation to con-sciousness and to community, or it can simply use up the life energy that was meant for learning how to love those unlike ourselves.

For me, having a spiritual director has been the closest experience of intercession or advocacy in community I have had. Each mission group in Seekers (there are six or eight at any given time) has a spiritual direc-tor who receives weekly written reports from each member, prays for that person, and responds to the report in writing. In addition, the spiritual director sees each person in the context of the group each week. When the group chooses someone who is respected and mature, the arrangement works well . . . as it has for me over the years. I have had only three different directors in the past twenty years, and with each one, I have felt held and known in a way that I believe would be impossible in a more casual arrangement. Because I have made an internal commitment to be as honest and unfinished in my written reports as I know how to be, I have felt loved in a way that includes my vices and my failings.

As a community, we trust the directors to be advocates and intercessors when needed. It does not always work, of course. Not every group chooses a wise director. Not every director is conscious and caring all the time. And sometimes we are just plain lazy in reporting. But my experience with different spiritual directors has let me know the power of having someone who will take my spiritual life seriously. It feels like a gift, not something I can earn or even deserve.

In our culture, I think we look to the legal profession for advocacy but do not expect others to intercede for us. Access to community, especially those that are closed associations, ethnic groups, or even churches, depends upon people who are willing to go out of their way as mentors, guides, or special autumn friends.

Confirmation

Transition into the communal setting of autumn friendship is often accompanied by signs or symbols that mark our release from prior claims and open the way to expanding new roles and relationships in the community. People within the community who speak "with authority" must provide some act of confirmation if we are to feel at home there.

After the elders of Bethlehem had completed their legal transaction, symbolized by the sandal exchange, the village women gave it a mythic interpretation by offering their communal blessing to the marriage of Ruth and Boaz: "May Yahweh make the woman who is to enter your House like Rachel and Leah who together built up the House of Israel"

(4:11 JB). They were referring to the sisters who provided the patriarch Jacob with twelve sons (see Genesis 29-30), who later led the twelve tribes of Israel. Such stories provide the tapestry of oral history that tells a people where they come from and who they are. By naming Rachel and Leah as the foremothers of Ruth, the women included Ruth in their lineage; they accepted the Moabite as one of their own.

The women's blessing also contained another curious reference: "Through the offspring the Lord gives you by this young woman, may your family be like that of Perez, whom Tamar bore to Judah" (4:12). The story of Judah and Tamar was another tale of tangled genealogy in which Tamar tricked her father-in-law, Judah, into fathering her child (actually twins). Tamar's husband had died, and his brother Onan had "spilled his seed on the ground" rather than preserve his brother's line through Tamar as levirate succession decreed (Genesis 38). By invoking Tamar, the women revealed another instance of God's way of moving beyond human laws and restrictions. They recalled the mysterious ways in which God had worked through property and ownership disputes in the past to bring vitality and new life to the covenant people. Fittingly, the book of Ruth ends with the genealogy of Boaz going back to Perez. By connecting Ruth with their history, the village women gave her an important place in their communal story. They spoke for God's creative inclusiveness.

The man's sandal and the women's blessing represent two kinds of confirmation given by the Bethlehem community. The men focused on control and property, what belonged to "me and mine," and the sandal exchange was a sign of their acceptance of Ruth under Mosaic Law. The women spoke with a communal voice of "us and ours," focused on the larger life force pulsing through the community. They directed their words to Naomi, as though to confirm her original hope and vision. Both the legal structure of rules and roles, and the mythic structure of blessing and confirmation, belong to the autumn season of friendship in community.

In my life, there was both a legal agreement—a sandal exchange— and a communal blessing to mark the beginning of my call to

Faith@Work. The "sandal exchange" occurred in December 1985, when I became the new president. For six months I had been running the office while a search committee looked for "a prior claimant" to the position. They had been looking for someone with at least ten years of parish experience and, in those days, that eliminated most women—including myself. Though I do not know what brought about the change, after examining a number of candidates, the committee offered me the position. Instead of a sandal, I had a letter and a paycheck to mark the transaction. It was a sign of our agreement, but not a deeply rooted symbol that would help me to tap into the archetypal energies I felt in this call.

The communal blessing came later in a surprising and spontaneous way. When the committee offered me the presidency, I simply continued going to the office as I had been doing for six months. My appointment would not be confirmed by the official "elders" until the board met several months later, and I felt the lack of any ritual ceremony to mark the shift in my status. However, during a weekend Faith@Work Women's Event, which coincided with the beginning of my new position, the women called me out of the circle to sit in a chair while they gathered around me for prayer. As each woman prayed for my role in guiding Faith@Work, she placed a construction paper hand on me. By the end, I had forty colorful hands stuck all over! It was a wonderful "laying on of hands" in the best religious tradition of ordaining one to ministry.

From Chicago, my friend Marianne sent a specially made clerical stole to mark the occasion. In gorgeous colors of peach and cream satin, it was both feminine and traditional in form. Since she and I met at a Faith@Work event nearly ten years earlier, she knew both the history and the uncertain future of the organization. She also knew that I had agonized over applying for ordination in a mainline denomination. And she knew the loss this choice would have meant for me, because I would have had to leave Seekers to pursue denominational ordination. When I chose Faith@Work, the stole was Marianne's tangible sign of blessing this alternative way of tending the garden of God's wider community beyond particular churches or denominations.

For Personal Reflection

Rules

- Think back to a community that you have been part of at some time in your life. Identify the "elders" or describe what you know of the informal power structure.
- Name a person who understood the nature of this community. What gift or key position did/does that person have there?
- Where do you find a sense of community today?

Intercession

- What barriers do you see that make entering community difficult?
- Who is (or might be) an intercessor for you?

Confirmation

- Who has (or could) confirm your entrance into community? What signs (role, title, job description) or symbols (images or objects) do you have of your acceptance into community? How would you describe those?
- How has your sense of belonging to a group been confirmed publicly?

For a Group

(15 minutes)

Call the circle together. Prepare an altar, light a candle, and begin with a prayer, song, chant, or silence. Then read the poem at the beginning of this chapter. Invite each person to add her symbol of summer friendship to the altar, saying a brief word about why she chose this symbol.

(10 minutes)

Use the poem to review main points of the chapter: complications of community, traditions and unspoken rules, roles and relationships unknown to newcomers, the importance of a translator or gateway person, and the value of a community's confirmation and acceptance.

(45 minutes)

In new triads, invite each person to speak about an autumn friendship:

- Name someone who has helped you negotiate the spoken and unspoken norms of a community or group. (Remember to define community broadly. It could be a family grouping, a social or political or church community, or maybe a sorority or service club.)
- Describe the community briefly and then focus on someone who was/is an autumn friend there.
- What qualities of your relationship made it an autumn friendship?

(20 minutes)

Return to the circle. Ask each person to retrieve her symbol and speak of her learning from this session on autumn friendship.

Ask the group to read chapter 6 for next week and bring another symbol of winter friendship.

Close with prayer and extinguish the candle.

Chapter 6

Winter Again
Sharing My Self

With child
Ruth waited
silent
still
alone
her body-self
a sacred chalice.

Her pledge
to Naomi
recalled
relived
realized.

I will go where you go,
live where you live.
Your people will be my people;
Your God, my God.
And where you die,
I will die.

*W*inter returns when external circumstances change, and we plunge into the unknown realm of spirit, of mystery, of death and birth. It is once again the season of "me" and "mine." With a winter friend we share what, in other seasons, we keep to ourselves: the inner world of self. For Naomi and Ruth, it was a time to revisit the pledge that Ruth made at the beginning of their journey together.

"I Will Go Where You Go"

The friendship between Ruth and Naomi shifted from autumn to winter when Ruth married Boaz, and the couple conceived a child. From the community interplay of legal discussion and women's blessing, Ruth withdrew into ritual seclusion, and Naomi took charge of the new household, claiming her role as family matriarch. Few words are given in the biblical story to describe this winter season of Ruth's life. The narrator simply reported, "The Lord enabled her to conceive, and she gave birth to a son" (4:13). But we do know that nine months passed, and life for the two friends would never be the same again.

The long gestation period was a time of stillness and darkness for the child, whose very presence gave Ruth a new identity as a mother and shifted her relationships with Naomi, with Boaz, and with the community as well. It was a very different winter season from the unprotected trek that the two women had made together from Moab to Bethlehem. This time they could rest safely in winter solitude, turning inward, musing and pondering without many words. It was a time of solitary reflection, sorting the past, and dreaming their new future together.

Having once received the pledge from Ruth to "go where you go," Naomi was now in a position to reciprocate. This time it was Naomi's turn to go with Ruth into the new territory of motherhood, sheltered and secure. The circumstances of their friendship now were quite different from finding food for survival. They would be getting used to a new home that would probably be theirs until one or the other died. They had time to explore a different way of walking together in their relationship, sharing time and tasks before the child's birth would give objective reality to their mothering roles.

Naomi had borne her sons as a young woman in her home community and then had been forced to leave Bethlehem with Elimelech just to survive. In contrast, Ruth was older, matured by events and decisions that followed a decade of childless marriage and widowhood, and was now living in a land full of promise. She had made her own decision to leave her homeland. Her independence was marked by a total separation from her mother, community, religion, land, and language when she decided to leave Moab and go with Naomi to Bethlehem.

But now Ruth had to shift from the independence of working hard in the male world of the grain fields to the patient waiting for her child to come when it would. So the two women entered Ruth's emerging motherhood together, each bringing their different life stages and experience to yet another winter season in their relationship. Their shared commitment—"I will go where you go"—is a winter statement of walking together, parallel but not joined, exploring some inward terrain with terror or wonder.

Giving priority to a winter friendship takes more attention than other relationships because winter friends share a more solitary space. Intuitions overlap. Winter friends may work together with a common goal, but they do not make demands, are not intrusive, and do not require constant reassurances. Small gestures of thoughtfulness substitute for words, and an atmosphere of waiting together sets the mood for winter friends. Often they are bound together by a crisis—illness, death of a parent or spouse, job loss—or the long gestation of a child whose birth will change everything for the parents. Winter friends hold the mystery of seeds and hidden hope between them.

For longtime friendships, particularly those with a strong spring-autumn dimension, winter is a time of testing, even confusion, over unexpected distance or silence. One person may be facing a winter crisis while the other is caught up in the whirl of autumn celebrations. Sensitivity to those differences can stretch or deepen a friendship, but we all know people who simply cannot walk with us in our seasons of hardship. It takes a level of maturity to weather the winter season if it has not been part of the landscape two friends have shared before.

Because we tend to live with overfull schedules, it is difficult to take the time just to BE together. That is why a common activity, such as training for a marathon or commuting together, can provide space for this less-verbal season to develop. One way to tend a winter friendship is to go away together, attend a retreat or conference where someone else will make decisions about schedule and meals, and you can simply be with each other. Exchanging poems, letters, drawings, or even favorite music can also speak from the depths of one to another.

If we have no language for our winter waiting time, we may feel depressed or isolated. But if we understand that winter is a resting time—a pause between sounds, a space between forms, a time of letting go before life rises once again—then we can welcome the winter season and look for winter friends. If we have shared a winter cycle with someone once before, that friendship may revive when the season comes around again.

I have noticed that whenever my own life brushes against death in some way, I reach out for Marianne because I know she will not recoil from my groping speech and frequent silences. Because she has walked with me through surgery and other losses, called when I could not, and named some of the hurts that might have driven us apart, I trust her not to shame my naked soul. I believe she would say the same. Although I have been blessed with a close and long-term marriage, there are things about being a woman in this world at this time that I can share with Marianne and not with my husband. Our impulses to reach for the phone and call just to talk often reveal some deeper stream that is already flowing beneath the surface of our words.

Like Ruth's period of gestation, winter friendships can also shelter new birth as it develops. Years ago, Marianne and I spent a week at Lake Michigan together. A summer storm made the lakeside cabin a refuge while waves lashed at the seawall and rain pelted the windows, surrounding us with primal sound and fury. She was studying for her licensing exams, and I was working on my first book. We kept silence all morning, then donned our slickers and walked in the cold spray before finding a place for dinner and some conversation. We expected sunshine and relaxation, but we were chilled and damp all week. Somehow, though, the weather was perfect for our winter friendship. It encouraged us to stay inside and be still together at a time when both of us were birthing new parts of ourselves.

More recently, Marianne and I have been part of a Crone group that meets twice a year with Jungian analyst Marion Woodman to explore dimensions of aging. The long drive from Chicago to London, Ontario, provides a time and space to let words arise out of silence. As we begin to share some of the realities of our aging bodies, changes in health and work patterns of our husbands, and other things that we have been thinking about since the last time we went, the car time becomes an unexpected gift of "walking" together.

"I Will Live Where You Live"

Living where another lives has a double meaning: to dwell in the same external place and to share an internal sense of aliveness. Winter friends can do both. They can accommodate differences of temperament and style to share a living space (though it may be temporary). They can also share some important love—such as art or running or prayer—that feeds a deeper longing. Discovering what brings life to our souls through interaction with another is characteristic of winter friendship. Sharing that nourishment means revealing our very source of life, living in a spiritual womb-space together.

Ruth had once pledged to live wherever Naomi was going to live, but at the end of the story, Naomi joined Ruth in a place that Ruth provided through her marriage to Boaz. The two friends had endured hardship together; now they shared the plenty together. They were wrapped together in the same physical house and nourished by the same spiritual source.

Ruth's pregnancy drew her focus inward, to her body. After ten years of childless marriage to Mahlon, and the hard seasons of widowhood with Naomi, suddenly Ruth had both safety and comfort she had not known before. As the child grew silently within her, Ruth would have known approval and acceptance by the other women of the village. Yet, as an active and self-reliant woman, the gestation period must have been difficult for her because it was so unfamiliar. Resting and receiving were not postures Ruth had assumed before.

Naomi, too, was pregnant with new life. Instead of dying old and alone and poor, she was in the process of becoming a grandmother, something she had wanted very much. After returning to Bethlehem, Naomi had grown in speech and imagination, as though her own body were "waking up." Because of Ruth's course of action, Naomi had really begun to live again. Now Naomi had tangible proof that her life, and Elimelech's line, were not going to be snuffed out after all. Together, Naomi and Ruth began to create a space in their relationship for the new life that was coming to each of them.

Like Ruth, we also turn inward to be "at home" in our bodies in the winter seasons of our lives. We pull away from friends and family, away from the extroverted communal activities of autumn periods, to replenish the solitary wellsprings of the soul. Winter is an introverted season, although we may remain functional and gregarious in public.

Winter friends draw sustenance from a common spiritual source, sharing some purpose or mutual need. Winter friends may be widows who work together on a church project, or young women who share a first apartment in the city to keep expenses down. Winter friends may "live together" as they endure common experience of hardship or share some inward pain.

In contrast to summer friendships, which are full of intense conversation and new activity, winter friends are more likely to share the sounds and smells of ordinary activity, such as cooking meals, without putting their thoughts into words. While the boundaries of "you" and "me" are still distinct, as in summer friendships, the environment is different: Winter friends have come inside and are contained by a surrounding spirit, which provides nourishment for them both.

Living where another lives can be frightening, as well as affirming, because the intention during this season is to be alone. As the eldest of three sisters, I was raised to be self-sufficient and resourceful in times of need. But as another winter season arrived in my life with a shift in my mother's health, I noticed an increasing desire to spend unstructured time with each of my sisters. After my father died in 1987, the three of us had begun a more intentional pattern of visiting my mother in Bellingham, Washington, from the different places we were living: Pueblo, Colorado; Kalamazoo, Michigan; and Washington, D.C.—but we never came at the same time. Then, in 2000, Mother fell and broke her arm. She needed help to wash, dress, and feed herself. Her need plunged all three of us into a winter season because the shadow of death moved quickly over the landscape.

At first we took turns staying with her in her retirement facility apartment. Then it became obvious that she needed more help than we could provide from long distance, so she moved into assisted living. Problem-solving for Mother became the external reason we needed to talk with each other, but something else was at work, too. I think we felt a deep visceral bond that was not obvious during the busy years of raising children. Finally, although her doctor thought she might not survive the move to a higher altitude, my mother accepted my youngest sister's invitation to move to Colorado. Barbara and I arranged for the move, rented a van, and checked out the legal ramifications if she should die on the trip. The three of us set out for a new place together, and the literal choice for life together became a spiritual journey.

Not only did Mother survive, but she is thriving! More contact with family, better food, more sunshine, and a new doctor who has taken her off most of her medications have given my mother a new lease on life. Just as important to me, though, is the gift of winter friendship that this transition has given me with my sisters. We have dipped into a common well of living water and found each other as adults.

"Your People Will Be My People"

At the physical level, Naomi's people could never be Ruth's people, but the child of Ruth and Boaz would make the younger woman part of Naomi's family heritage. The child would move Naomi and Ruth's friendship from a chosen commitment into the primitive bonding of blood and family. But at the spiritual level, Naomi's people were already Ruth's family. It was a time for developing her trust and faith in the Jewish tribal customs, which Ruth had long ago accepted through her commitment to Naomi. As she gave herself to Naomi's people and carried in her womb a child who belonged among them, images of her own mother and her own childhood may have surrounded her as well. It would have been a time for remembering the past and dreaming the future for herself and her child. Like an animal in hibernation, sharing the time and space with other women, Ruth herself became the integration of her past and her present. What she had intended with her will and her words—"your people will be my people"—was now becoming a reality in both spirit and flesh.

In the beginning, it had been Naomi who had spoken so fervently about having a child, because it would ensure Elimelech's line and give her a place among her own people. Ruth had never voiced any particular interest in marriage or childbearing, although she had asked Boaz to redeem them, thereby offering herself to him. Unlike most of the women in that day, Ruth seemed more independent, operating by force of will instead of fitting into the collective patterns of childbearing that Naomi wanted. Now Ruth was joined to Naomi's people by marriage and by birth, birthing herself among them through this child. There would be no going back even if Naomi died. This child meant that Naomi's people were Ruth's own.

The archetypal image of pregnancy as a seed of hope reflects how a winter friendship holds the potential for spiritual renewal in the soil of two people with a deep spiritual connection. The potential birth is a third party to the relationship, giving shape and form to a story belonging to both partners. What shape and form this story takes cannot be controlled by either partner. It must simply be held and nurtured between them—a gift from beyond themselves, the fruit of friendship and commitment, of eternal renewal, even when death draws close in some way.

Identifying "my people" is an extension and expansion of understanding "my self." Winter friends who share the same internal community can give birth to "a new people" out of their commitment to each other, rather than searching for admittance to an external community created by others. When we internalize a sense of belonging to a community—belonging to their history and ultimately their highest values or God—then we reach a level of security and internal freedom that may allow us to share that heritage with others. Just as the cycles of nature hold out the image of winter rest and fallow fields to gather energy for a new season of growth, winter friends save us from despair when we come to the edge of our mortality. As we become conscious of depth connections in our winter friendships, we will need to name and celebrate the fruits of the relationship who give form and substance to "our'people" in the world.

When I consider the question of mingling internal communities, I come back to my relationship with Peter, who is both my beloved husband and my winter friend. The fruit of our relationship has been conceived, birthed, sheltered, taught, and released again and again as our relationship has matured in different communities. Sharing the same space at home and the same bed at night encourages our winter bond. Coming to the mysteries of death and life in worship at Seekers has helped us trust God's purpose for our lives, even when we could not see it. Our life together and separately has given birth to images that carry us through other seasons in our relationship.

I have learned that there is a big difference between saying the words of Ruth's pledge—"your people will be my people"—and living the words together. When I first said this pledge at our wedding, I took the words literally to mean that Peter's community would replace my own: His name would replace the one I had grown up with, his parents would substitute for mine, and his work would provide our community context. And, in some ways, that happened. However, over the years the deeper spiritual source of our winter friendship has provided a sense of belonging to a larger human family than either his parents or mine, and we have shared the essence of our relationship as we have opened our home to others, creating "our people" in the process. Instead of having community made for us by others, we are continuing to invite community into being out of our winter friendship.

"Your God Will Be My God"

Entering someone else's belief system means sharing thoughts and values behind the descriptive words and stories of their faith. But the biblical covenant goes even further to say that we can actually be in relationship with Yahweh, the living God. Beyond the Mosaic Law, God is understood to be the source of life, the central "I am who I am" (Exodus 3:14).

If Naomi's God had blessed the marriage of Ruth and Boaz by causing Ruth to conceive this child, then Ruth's faithful pursuit of this redeeming act had brought Naomi back to a living relationship with the covenant again. Following the death of her two sons, Naomi had felt cursed by God, or at least felt that God's blessing had been withdrawn from her family. Naomi's core of faith had been stripped of all wish-dreams to a simple act of will—choosing life—in order to make the long desert journey from Moab to Bethlehem. Now Naomi's faith took on flesh and blood once again with the sign of blessing in Ruth's womb.

Ruth, too, must have felt God's blessing on her union with Boaz when she conceived a child so quickly. But as she became part of the covenant people through this child, she also knew that her full acceptance by them lay in bearing a son, not a daughter, to continue Elimelech's line. Unlike nearby goddess-worshiping tribes (such as her own in Moab), Israel was a patriarchal society, and property passed to male descendants. Although the Hebrews regarded fecundity as a positive sign of Yahweh's presence, the priests and judges of Israel rejected fertility rites and household gods when Ruth's story was circulated after the Babylonian Exile. It was the ongoing *relationship* with God that made Naomi's God different from the household gods with which Ruth probably grew up.

For women today, the Judeo-Christian preference for males continues to be a stumbling block for many. The idea that Ruth's importance to God's story through the people of Israel rests on the gender of her child is repugnant to us because it implies that women are valuable only if they bear children, especially male children. Certainly there are plenty of examples of that patriarchal attitude among Jewish and Christian congregations today.

But the story of Ruth is much more than just a woman's name in a genealogical list of David and of Jesus (Matthew 1:5). The complexity of the story of her relationship with Naomi suggests that the image of God's presence is being carried and nurtured by these two women as they lived through the changing seasons of friendship together. Ruth's story reveals a God of relationship that goes far beyond the literal birth of a child and the gender preference of a people. Its mythic power comes from moving beyond sexual stereotypes.

The friendship between Ruth and Naomi actually is a dynamic portrayal of the nature of God: inviting, inclusive, and expansive. This God joins Ruth and Naomi, drawing them toward life before the older woman was even conscious of the bond between them. This God beckons Ruth with an invitation to faithful commitment, rather than subservient sacrifice. This God responds to the independent choice of a "foreigner." This God is quite beyond the conventional images of a patriarchal Old Testament judge. The God revealed by this story is rooted in the history of the Israelites but not confined to their cultural expression.

At different times in Ruth and Naomi's relationship, one supplied what the other could not. Without the perseverance and physical energy of Ruth, they might not have survived. Without the vision of Naomi, the provision of God might have gone unnoticed. We, too, need the different gifts that individuals bring to a relationship. We need the different perspectives of age and experience. Through our differences, we bring our combined life experience, positive and negative, to the words of faith recorded in the Bible, and then we can begin to understand the meaning and purpose and interconnection of all life. We catch sight of God's vision for the diversity of creation and for the part that we have in it.

The pledge to take on somebody else's God is a troubling one for me, even though I believe that we all see partial images and know God only imperfectly. My life experience has convinced me that no church or denomination or faith tradition fully describes the mystery at the heart of creation, but I do trust the biblical revelation of a God who walks with us. I know the presence of Christ and have put my roots down in a religious community to follow Jesus in the way I relate to others. Like Ruth, I look for others who are more experienced in living their faith. Like Naomi, I know that I am sometimes a guide for others. My best friends are those such as Marianne who share their search for God with me.

"Where You Die, I Will Die"

For Ruth, the period between the baby's conception and birth must have been a time of hope—and a time of dying to her old independent self. She was leaving the pre-pregnant separate individual person whom she knew herself to be in order to begin a lifelong connection with the stranger growing inside of her body. She would, in fact, allow the child to come between herself and Naomi. At the same time, of course, the child would solidify her relationship with Naomi.

Not only did Ruth have to face the symbolic death of her separate self, but she faced the actual possibility of death as well. Although Ruth had a strong, healthy, farmworker's body, she lived close to nature and would have known the many dangers of childbirth. For one who lived close to the land, evoking death as the ultimate pledge of loyalty would signify all that she had to give. The confluence of birth and death brought her to the edge of mystery and divine presence.

For Naomi, the question of death had a different meaning than it did for Ruth. Naomi was older, and she had already lost a husband and two sons. She was not the one at risk any longer, and she knew from experience that she could survive. This time it was Naomi's turn to accompany Ruth on a fearful and dangerous path, assuring her that she would protect the child if anything happened to Ruth. As winter friends, they could face the possibility of death without hiding from it or leaving one another.

Although we modern women have pushed death to the periphery of our consciousness, it still haunts our humanness. If we do not block our fear of dying or try to avoid the loneliness and despair that comes with certain winter seasons—what St. John of the Cross called "the dark night of the soul"—then we can participate in the dying of old forms, old relationships, and outdated patterns. With our winter friends, we can explore the inner terrain of the spirit and share the silent world of gestation as new life takes shape inside, before it is birthed in the world.

Dying is hardly the stuff of friendship for most people. Yet it was the bond that initially drew me close to Marianne when we met in 1978, and closer to my sisters at the time of my father's death in 1987. I have also learned about the kind of holy space of timeless death that can happen on a silent retreat. Twice a year, sixteen members from the Seekers community go on silent retreat together. It is like an extended Eucharist, seeing each other as the "body of Christ" without the usual covering of our words, tasting the elixir of spirit and new life in different ways from the same container. We intentionally spend those weekends without words (except for what the retreat leader offers), sharing the experience of God's mysterious presence. There is a sense in which we are in God together, as though we were sharing a womb-space. Somehow, silence is an experience of death and being loved at the same time. We are stripped of individual preconceptions about God and about how our lives ought to be. I always come back cleansed and surprised by the time of rest, with a sense of renewal that comes from giving myself to the experience of intentional silence.

Winter is the season of wonder, of holy waiting and meditation on the limits of our mortality. Winter is the season of endings, of grief and loss—feelings that arise as a measure of how much we have loved and our capacity for caring. To all outward appearances, the winter season is a time to be alone, to be a friend to one's own self. But as we do that, we discover the common core of our humanity—aliveness itself—mediated through our flesh. In silence we can approach the possibility of death and reflect on those mysterious inner forces that bring new birth out of death or collapse or tragedy. Time alone becomes time shared with others at the deeper level of mourning, wonder, and mystery.

For Personal Reflection
"I Will Go Where You Go"

- Consider winter as a time of commitment to the unknown or unspoken parts of yourself. What image or color would you use to describe yourself in winter?
- Name a winter friend with whom you feel safe enough to share your inner self. Describe your friendship nonverbally—with an image, colors, or drawing.
- What new parts of your life have been birthed in the shelter of this friendship?

"I Will Live Where You Live"

- Are there colors, textures, sounds, or stories that make you feel specially "at home"?
- What "dwelling place" do you share, or have you shared, with a winter friend?

"Your People Will Be My People"

- What has been born of your dreaming with a winter friend?
- How do you contribute, or have you contributed, to a "new people" or a new community out of a winter friendship?

"Your God Will Be My God"

- How do you experience God? Nonverbally describe "your God"—with an image, colors, or drawing.

- How has your understanding of God changed through a winter friendship?

"Where You Die, I Will Die"
- What is your experience with dying and new birth through a winter friendship?
- What do you need to let die in order for some new life in a friendship to be born?
- What new life has come out of shared silence for you?

For a Group

(15 minutes)
Call the circle together. Prepare an altar, light a candle, and begin with a prayer, song, chant, or silence. Then read the poem at the beginning of this chapter. Invite each person to add her symbol of winter friendship to the altar, saying a brief word about why she chose this symbol.

(10 minutes)
Use the poem to review main points of the chapter: winter as a season of waiting, pondering, and revisiting old commitments from a more seasoned vantage point.

(45 minutes)
In new triads, invite each person to speak about a winter friendship. Offer these questions for consideration:

- Have you ever accompanied someone without knowing where it would take you?
- Name some of the fruits—positive and negative—of living with another person.
- How have you shared your understanding of God with someone over time?
- How has your experience with or understanding of death impacted a friendship?

(20 minutes)

Return to the circle. Ask each person to retrieve her symbol from the altar and speak of her learning from this session on winter friendship.

Ask the group to read chapter 7 for next week and bring another symbol of spring friendship.

Close with prayer and extinguish the candle.

Chapter 7

Spring Returns
Birthing New Life

In we-ness of spring
Naomi took the child
renewed
reborn
a family restored.

"The child
will be a comfort
in your old age . . ."
the women sang, and
"Don't forget Ruth
who loves you
and is more
to you than seven sons."

The men kept account
    of the fathers:
Boaz succeeded
        Elimelech and Mahlon
as father to Obed . . .
to David . . .
to Joseph . . .
to Jesus.
Their record was clear,
generations all named
but they couldn't
keep Yahweh
contained.

*B*irthing new parts of ourselves and new initiatives into the world continues to happen throughout life, and our friend-ships midwife the changes, releasing the past and welcoming the future. As the biblical story draws to a close, the particular relation-ship between Ruth and Naomi almost disappears, subsumed in the larger sweep of song and myth. The image of birthing takes on a dimen-sion beyond the personal story of Ruth and Naomi. Safety and trust produce an archetypal image of internal integration. Nurture and love invite new cultural interpretations. Language and memory provide con-tinuity for future generations.

Integration

The birth of Obed, whose name means "serving," marks the final phase of the relationship between Ruth and Naomi. Obed fed the hunger in Naomi's soul that could not be filled with food alone. He linked Naomi's singular decision to return to Bethlehem with the larger con-text of the covenant promise. He restored the family line, and he served the people of Israel as a sign of God-with-us instead of a God who vis-ited every so often. Indeed, Obed was the precursor of another babe who would be born in Bethlehem from David's family line.

The story says that "Naomi took the child to her own bosom and she became his nurse" (4:16 JB). Figuratively, she became the Mother. As she drew the child close to her own body, she became his guardian, and they became a primary pair. Naomi embodied the image of Yahweh as she drew him under her protective wing. She had been transformed by this birth from a dried-up old crone into a numinous figure of the Wise Woman.

If the story had ended with Ruth giving birth to a son, it would have been a conventional story in which the younger woman "won" by find-ing a wealthy husband to father her child, and the older woman "lost" because she had outlived her usefulness once her friend found a man to marry. However, Ruth seems to disappear from the story at this point, as though she had completed her female task by bearing a son. But the women of the village remember Ruth to Naomi as the "daughter-in-law, who loves you" (4:15). Their role was to weave the story, to name what had happened from a larger perspective. Ruth had not disappeared from the collective consciousness of the Bethlehem women!

The image of a spring dyad—of Mother and Child—speaks of safety, nurture, and developing forms of language. Between spring friends, safety becomes trust, nurture grows into mutual love, and language provides both memory and hope. All of that is carried by the image of Naomi holding the child to her aged breast: Bonding is forged through commitment rather than simple biology; the past and future coalesce.

As women, we can bring the dedication of Ruth and the vision of Naomi to the creative work of birthing our own relationships. The pairings of Naomi and Ruth, Ruth and Obed, and Obed and Naomi provide a biblical image that is rich with generative possibilities. Ruth's courage and self-sufficiency provide an ancient image for our work in the world as strong, capable women. Naomi's determined hope for family and children holds out a model for believing in our visions. And Obed's long-awaited birth embodies hope for new life that will grow out of trusted relationships.

Most of us enter adult friendship from a preferred stance, either as the independent Naomi, dependent Obed, or interdependent Ruth. I have usually begun a friendship from the stance of Naomi. As the eldest child in my biological family, there was not much space for being a dependent and needy child. In an effort to please my parents during the chaotic years of World War II, I learned to "stand on my own two feet" and not ask for help. I maintained that independent stance in my friendships as Peter and I moved from one Moab to another during his Army career. I had always been cautious about committing myself, as Ruth did, to another woman friend until I met Marianne. The timing and circumstances for both of us seemed right for a mutual exchange of Mother and Child needs when our friendship began. Over the years, our friendship has grown, stretched, withered, and sprouted new seeds. We have been intentional about feeding our relationship across the miles. We have been intentional about visiting, attending family celebrations, addressing issues of envy and jealousy when they arose, and attending growth seminars together each year. We have worked at integrating changes, and I think we have come around to another spring season as crones.

Interpretation

Being included in a community means being included in the stories or mythology by which a community describes itself. Interpretive stories give people a way to understand what is happening to them. In America, for example, we have grown up with the stories of our country's welcome to "the tired and the poor" from many lands. Most of us can name an immigrant ancestor who came looking for a better life.

The biblical tradition takes many forms, of course, but a central premise is that it is possible for an individual (and a people) to have a direct and ongoing relationship with the divine source of all creation, with God. When we belong to a community that celebrates that divine presence symbolically in worship, we have a framework to hold the unconscious as well as conscious forces at work in our lives. Belonging to a bigger story than the one we can create for ourselves makes it possible to let go of what we already "know" and trust that something new will arrive from the mysterious source of the universe.

Like a collective mother's voice, the women of Bethlehem retold the story of Naomi's spiritual journey from a woman's standpoint. Years earlier, they had witnessed the promise of Naomi's spring marriage to Elimelech, followed by the summer emptiness of famine and her departure from Bethlehem. They had greeted her return with a question: "Could this be Naomi?" Then they gave Naomi a place to name her winter despair and watched while the cycle of seasons began again: spring friendship with Ruth, summer searching for food, autumn acceptance into the village property structure, and winter waiting for the child. Now the community of women rejoiced once more in the coming of spring to Naomi's friendship with Ruth through the birth of

Obed. The women of the village—not the village elders—named the child and provided interpretive language for Obed's role in the story.

Even though the women of Bethlehem upheld the traditional value of bringing children into the community, they were able to re-interpret the cultural preference for males and celebrate the birthing power of friendship between Naomi and Ruth: "[She] is better to you than seven sons," they proclaimed (4:15). According to the male value system, no woman could be as valuable as a son, let alone "seven sons." But the women told a different story: They recognized Ruth's love for Naomi as the source of new life. Their blessing was a remarkable re-interpretation of official community values. They re-interpreted the past and provided language for a new theology of life based on love more than law. Their version became the biblical story, the carrier of God's truth.

When I first read Judith Duerk's book *Circle of Stones,* I found myself yearning for the circle of women she describes, women who could help me interpret my experience from a larger perspective, women who could help me find my place in God's sacred story of creation. Although women give birth individually, often aided by the midwifing of a friend, the ability to find meaning and value for our lives depends upon the stories that link our birthings with a larger interpretive framework. Among women who understand that the biological urge to have children is, at the core, a drive to bring spirit into form, the celebration of bringing all forms of new life into the world is an important aspect of being female together. The women who help us name and interpret our birthings have a priestly function and express God's call to women beyond bearing children.

The women's ministry of Faith@Work has again and again been a place for me to hear the Bethlehem song of celebrating women's friendships. I have often come to a Women's Event as Naomi, with difficulty celebrating a woman's love as being more important than achieving status or control in the external world of work and material possessions—our equivalent of having "seven sons."

Recently I came to a Faith@Work Women's Event as just one more obligation on my crowded calendar. I had led this particular retreat design several times before and could not imagine that anything new would come from doing it again. I was also preoccupied with other things. Like Naomi, I felt full of responsibilities and empty of joys.

As we do for all Women's Events, the leadership team met ahead of the retreat to prepare ourselves for the event. The women on this team gave me a safe place to talk about the pictures I had brought to share as a part of the retreat process, pictures from my childhood: my mother, sisters, and grandmothers. As I talked about ways these women affect my life today, I began to weep. The women in my small group simply waited and listened, hearing me into speech as I struggled to find language for my feelings. Nobody tried to give advice or even sympathize with me. Having a safe place to name the truth about those relationships made it holy ground. Being able to see the women in my family through the lens of who God is calling me to be gave it a different interpretive dimension.

One woman in the group was someone with whom I had worked when she was Chair of the Faith@Work Board. She is about ten years older than I am and lives with the constant fragility of her husband's health. Nan and I walked in the early morning hours, and she voiced her yearning for solitude, for space and time alone to face the next phase of her inner journey. We talked about the image of seasons in life and in relationships. As I listened, I felt myself shift from Naomi's role to Ruth's. I simply said, "I can walk with you . . . at a distance . . . so you'll have a winter friend and not have to take care of me, too." Somehow it was enough. I let go of my weary separateness for the loving interdependence of Ruth. Through the dynamic of the Women's Event, the words we shared in our small group, and the particular conversation Nan and I shared, I could hear the pulse of life and name the value of women's friendship once again.

Sharing my story with other women has helped me look at the strands between my present experience and internal voices from the past that denigrate intuitive and personal ways of knowing truth in favor of logic and control—our equivalent of the law. Even though I cannot always hear the interpretive song of the Bethlehem women celebrating the love of Ruth "who is better to you than seven sons," I know where to go when I have lost touch with that music. My ears are most open to hear a new song, a new interpretation of God's love, when a particular friendship has produced a new dance of life between Naomi and Ruth.

Continuity

The men of Bethlehem, who were more concerned about family lines and property rights than about caring for two widows, contributed the final verses of the biblical narrative: an official listing of fathers and sons, showing the connection among Judah, Perez, Boaz, Obed, and the genealogy of King David (4:18-22). Even today, some scholars maintain that the story of Ruth is included in the biblical canon only because she was the grandmother of King David; others see it as a love poem rather than a radical image of God. But in the details of those genealogy lists, we can find clues in the male system of records that support a more fluid and open story of how God works in the lives of ordinary people. Elimelech disappears in favor of Boaz. It's not about keeping the history straight!

Though unnamed in the historical list, Ruth's place in David's family line is clear. Without her, Boaz would not be there. Family continuity would have been disrupted, and God's larger story would have been less colorful. Ruth was a foreigner, one of the forbidden mates sprinkled through the Hebrew Testament, as though God purposely reminded men not to get too legalistic about their bloodlines. Ruth chose into God's plan before it became a matter of official record. Through her commitment to Naomi—and to God through Naomi's stubborn faith—Ruth became part of a long family line that included Tamar, Rahab, Bathsheba, and Mary, the foremothers of Jesus (Matthew 1:1-16). These women, and unnamed others, gave birth to hope for all those at the margins of society because they chose life rather than let social rules dictate how they should live.

As women reading this biblical story, we can marvel at the mysterious and creative power of God that refuses to be confined by the boundaries of law and language. The stories of Tamar and Rahab reveal a creative God who was not confined by the law or rigorous morality. The wildness of God's way often comes as a surprise to those who think we have tamed the truth into being good, right, or fair. These women reveal a scandalous force at work in the world, creating new vitality out of the limitations of time, space, and finite being. This God brings life out of death through women who dare to take their own creative energy seriously.

As part of the biblical record, Ruth's story stands as a parable of God's mercy and generativity through a female friendship. Where human hopes foundered on the barrenness of Naomi's sons, God's story grew from the seed of Naomi's faith, producing hope in Ruth and ultimately hope in a people. The women of Bethlehem were able to see that Ruth's love was a source of new life. As they incorporated the story of Ruth's love for Naomi into their cultural myths, the women provided an expansive view of God's intention and purpose in history. These two women dared to live as though their lives mattered to each other and to God.

In the end, all birthing is an act of faith and a commitment to life. The story of Naomi and Ruth gives birth again and again, in ever-widening circles. The relationship between Ruth and Naomi opened the way to Boaz and Obed. The song of women in Bethlehem opened the way to a new interpretation of God. And the written record opened the way to God's larger plan for the birth of Christ.

Opening to new birth is probably the quality that I look for most in a friendship because it is central to my faith and understanding of God. I sensed it in Marianne when we first met. I see it in her mother, who just had her one-hundredth birthday. I flew out to Chicago to help with a large family gathering for Grandma Marie's centennial celebration. She said to anyone who was listening, "I ask God 'Have you forgotten me?' and God says 'No, Marie. It's not time yet.' So I'll just wait. I have a good life, but I'm ready to go." I was deeply moved because I know her story. She came to America as an immigrant from Sweden to be a maid. She never had much education, married another Swedish immigrant, raised three children in downtown Chicago, and worked hard all her life. Seeing Marianne's mother sitting in a rocking chair, holding her ten-day-old great grandson, Soren, with her face alight with love, I had a sense of Naomi and the generations of faith of which I am a part. Because Marianne's mother approaches death with a sense of anticipation and new birth, it helps me trust Marianne even more with the next seasons of our friendship. Naming the history between us has been an important reminder that life is made of many seasons, that pain and death can be redeemed, and that spring will always follow winter. When we can see the continuity of the past, we can hope for the future.

For Personal Reflection

Integration

- Identify the role that seems most natural to you at the beginning of a friendship: Naomi's independence, Obed's dependence, or Ruth's interdependence.
- Describe a friendship in which you have experienced all three roles over time. How does that friendship relate to your current sense of internal integration?

Interpretation

- Where are the women who help you interpret the value of your own experience? (Consider books, media, friends, groups within your community.)
- Describe a time or season when you have heard their "Bethlehem song," interpreting facts with new meaning.

Continuity

- Go back to the circle of friendship that you drew in chapter 1. Add additional names of friends in each season, giving thanks for their differences and the qualities that they bring out in your life.
- Go back to the timeline that you drew in chapter 2. Add symbols for new life that you see emerging, giving thanks for your birthing power.

For a Group

(15 minutes)
Call the circle together. Prepare an altar, light a candle, and begin with a prayer, song, chant, or silence. Then read the poem at the beginning of this chapter. Invite each person to add her symbol of spring friendship to the altar, saying a brief word about why she chose this symbol.

(10 minutes)
Use the poem to review main points of the chapter: interpretation, integration, and continuity

(45 minutes)
In new triads, invite each person to speak about a spring friendship. Offer these questions for consideration:

- How has a spring friend helped you interpret your life in a new way?
- How has a spring friend helped you integrate difficult or painful segments of your life?
- How has a spring friend helped you find a thread of continuity that you had not seen before?

(20 minutes)
Return to the circle. Ask each person to retrieve her symbol from the altar and speak of her learning from this session on spring friendship.

Ask the group to read chapter 8 for next week and bring something that symbolizes divine presence for them.

Close with prayer and extinguish the candle.

Chapter 8

Seasons of Friendship with God

The spiral never stops.
Like seasons rolling toward
each equinox we find ourselves
anew with friends
re-birthing God again.

At first
a muted sea surrounds us
heard as heartbeat
of the source
Great Mother's.

Winter comes
and human systems crumble
but consciousness survives
by each one claiming
what she needs for life—

one ready to face death alone,
another set to leave her mother's
     home.

Then cradled,
we are rocked
beloved
and fed
on spirit food.

Come drought
or simply growth inside
the cozy pair
gives way to search for call
or form in work
and words.

If seed of spring
is dropped
where summer heat
and winter seep
can nourish roots
that feed on deeps,
then friendships grow to harvest
and the fruits of friendship
keep us through the dark
of winter cold
. . . until
day comes again.

W e could view the story of Naomi and Ruth simply as a tale of miraculous circumstances that resulted in the birth of King David's grandfather. But if we look at the deeper implications—how their friendship with God changed in each season—then we can focus the polarizing lens of the story on our changing relationships with God as well. In Naomi and Ruth's winter season, God was a protective womb, supporting new life until it could survive in the external world. In spring, God put a sheltering wing around them, providing safety for Ruth in the fields and for Naomi in the village. In summer, God seemed distant and hard, as though waiting for each one to risk safety and security for a larger goal. In autumn, God was manifested by the community with its ongoing history and traditions. And then the cycle began again, with the generative possibilities of God in human experience.

As an introvert, I feel more familiar with the summer and winter seasons of friendship with God. I know what to do in those more internal times. I rely on tradition and past experience to claim my inward relationship with God that will keep new life rising again. In spring and autumn, the more extroverted and sociable seasons, I am surprised by God's love and care through others, as though I do not deserve to be included. Extroverted friends bridge the isolation of my separateness and give flesh to the mysterious power of love.

Winter Gestation

A winter relationship with God begins with a simple decision to trust God's surrounding love and care, whether there is good evidence for it or not. The ability to do that may come out of life experience, or from biblical stories that inspire trust, such as the Exodus account or Naomi's journey. The image of a surrounding and nourishing God as the infusing source of life exists both in our biological memory of being in the womb and in the Genesis story of Adam and Eve in the Garden of Eden. Where experience and story meld, we sense our connection with creation at a deep level of being.

Like Naomi, we may have to live through one cycle of seasons before we realize that our relationship with God, and our images of God, change over time. Most of us begin with an image of God that is supposed to be all-seeing, all-knowing, and all-good. Then winter comes, and we either change our understanding of God . . . or die.

Initially, Naomi understood the meaning of her life as a woman in a conventional way: through childbearing and family perpetuation. Her path seemed to be a linear one from birth to death, from springtime youth to wintry age. Her early spring years in Bethlehem were marked by a new home and family. Summer came with famine and the journey to Moab in search of food. Autumn, the period of establishing the community of an extended family after Elimelech died, was marked by the addition of Orpah and Ruth to her household. Winter came when her sons died leaving no children. In her culture, Naomi's life was over.

Then Naomi discovered the power of God in herself, and she had a choice: She could respond to the urge for life or ignore it. She chose life by embarking on a journey homeward, toward Bethlehem. Her winter friendship with God began with this decision, a sheer act of will based

on mute faith. She needed to complete the journey of individuation—
the call to be creative throughout life—by reclaiming the faith of her
past as an independent single woman. In doing so, Naomi had to draw
on a spirit that went beyond what she had been taught, beyond the cultural belief that measured her value according to her ability to produce
sons. Moving beyond Mosaic Law and Hebrew culture, Naomi discovered the mystical flame of God's spirit inside. Acknowledging the curse
of childlessness that God apparently had put on her sons, Naomi was
courageous and stubborn enough to risk a solitary journey because she
dared to dream of being included in the covenant story once again.
Naomi's choice for her self was part of a fuller revelation of God's love
and intention for women.

Naomi began her journey to fill an emptiness in her soul, but she
did not have to reach Bethlehem before God's grace began to show. Her
closed circle of seasons was opened by Ruth's unilateral pledge of companionship. Naomi said "yes" to the possibility of relationship when she
stopped trying to dissuade Ruth from joining her on the desert journey
to Bethlehem. Like a woman discovering she is pregnant in her old age,
Naomi silently agreed to accept Ruth's presence and let it live within the
circle of her wintry soul.

God's accompanying presence was signaled by Ruth's commitment
and the uneventful journey they made around the Dead Sea. At the
point when all other sources of help and protection had been torn away,
God provided them with sustenance for their long journey through alien
territory. As in the Exodus story, God moved with them as spirit,
unnamed but not unknown. With each step of the way, both women
must have felt shielded, if not led.

In our extroverted and busy culture, there is little public attention
given to the gifts of winter friendship with God. We purchase privacy,
yet, on the whole, we do not like to spend long periods in quiet con-
templation or alone. We flee from pain, despair—even silence. We do
not want those periods of introspection. We avoid discomfort and try to
overcome interruptions. We want control over who will enter the gates
of our city or house or circle of friends. Many of us do not even like to

be reminded that conception is still a mystery, and childbearing itself requires a commitment to protect and nurture what we do not understand or control.

As women, we often avoid the inward journey of trusting God until it is forced on us by age or circumstances. A winter friend such as Ruth, someone with courage to make a commitment without needing much response, may catalyze the shift from external questions of role and survival to internal questions of self and direction. In retreat from the activities of more extroverted seasons, we can discover the power to trust God in prayer, journaling, body movement, or meditation. We may look death in the face and discover internal resources that we did not know were there. When we can live into the mysteries of a winter friendship with God, we may discover a surprising power to trust an inner spirit rooted in the core of "me," as Naomi did. We may discover the power to love without conditions, as Ruth did.

The presence of God surrounds my sense of self in the winter season. It is as close and supportive as the air I breathe . . . and just about as impersonal. Few people share my winter season of friendship with God. It is sustained by being alone, musing, meditating, walking, and wondering. I feel lost in darkness and inclined to self-pity. My dreams are infused by a river of spirit where images become shapes that move, shift, and reveal the fog of unconscious feeling. Every morning, I rise in the cold, silent house before dawn, sit with my journal to draw my dreams, wrestle with the lectionary readings, and pray for God's mercy as I read the newspaper. Centering prayer has become part of my daily practice, consciously repeating a simple mantra as I simply rest in God's nearness. Periodic silent retreats ground me in this season, creating space within for new life. Eucharist is a reminder of my winter friendship with God, full of the mystery of death and life.

In winter, I am alone . . . quiet . . . introspective.

In winter, God is my silent source . . . giving me time and space to know and understand my self.

Spring Encounter

The transition from gestation to birth marks the coming of spring in our relationship with God, as it does between friends. Internal changes are revealed in external form, and there is new energy, activity, and hope. Spring friendship with God is full of Easter energy. As we mid-wife and mother each other, we feel loved, nurtured, and needed, as the disciples of Jesus were. There is a sense of new possibilities, even lightness and humor, as we encounter the living God embodied in a human friendship.

Naomi and Ruth experienced the mutuality of caring for each other after they reached Bethlehem, and they encountered God's care as their needs were met providentially. Ruth faced into her fears of being molested in order to feed them both. Her willingness to risk her virtue—even her life—for the sake of their survival together evoked a blessing and a prayer from Naomi. They were ready to rely on God rather than seek a male protector. Together, they met a God who was close by, intimate, and caring.

The differences in their age, energy, and expectations were the stim-ulus for reaching beyond conventional patterns for their survival. One provided what the other needed, but neither was locked into the role of Mother or Child. Their needs met and joined. They shared their fears about Ruth's safety in the field, and they rejoiced together over the serendipitous provision of Boaz and his generosity, a sign Naomi recog-nized as God's parental care. Even the flirtatious bantering tone of Ruth's conversation with Boaz was, at another level, Ruth's encounter with God: trusting, easy, and comfortable.

There will be times in our lives when we need the mutual mother-ing that Naomi and Ruth gave to each other. We may reach for a friend-ship, a marriage, or a church home where we can feel safe and receive special attention and care. During those times, we may also look to God for nurture, shelter, and miraculous provisions. We will seek the active shepherding aspect of God instead of the mystery and silence of a win-ter prayer life. We will look for food and touch as a sign of God's par-enting presence. A childlike quality may even add a dimension of innocent playfulness to our spring friendship with God. We will want to feel welcomed, known, and loved, not challenged or called to serve. We will stay immature in our faith, however, if we want all spring and no winter in our friendship with God.

The power of spring birthing is strong in God's creation, which includes our bodies and our souls. We can claim the power of new birth beyond literal childbearing, in both aging and singleness. Birthing—physical and spiritual—occurs more easily with the affirmation and encouragement of a friend. If we find a mutually nourishing friendship to midwife our births, we will continue to claim God's power of creativity through us until the very edge of death. If we do not have spring friendships to nurse the inner child of new life, then we may become the dry and bitter crone that Naomi thought she was when she arrived back in Bethlehem. We do not have to be ashamed of our dependent spring periods, early or late in life. Birthing does not last forever, but during this season, we need warmth and caring to know that we are God's beloved child.

Spring gives us an opportunity to follow our inner sense of purpose developed over the winter season, and to find an outward encounter with another loving person who expands our hopes and energizes creation. As we encounter God in the kindness and compassion of human caring, new understandings of God's "tender mercies" are born.

For me, spring is a playful season, full of freshness and lively starts. Even God seems full of good humor, and my dreams are filled with puns in spring. Egg images abound. It is the season of whimsy. I am more likely to join other liturgical clowns in our church, interpreting the Gospel lesson with humor and pathos. In the spring season with God, I am eager to share my clown, "Cheap Grace," wearing her feathers and bubbles at church, Children's Hospital, or a special birthday party. It is a time of knowing that I can be loved and accepted even when I am playing the fool. But spring is also the hardest season for me because I have the least control over myself and others. I cannot *earn* the joy that comes unexpectedly, surprisingly, as "good news" from the least likely sources.

My spring friendship with God is also the season of grace and trust, of hearing Jesus call me by name to come as a little child, to get into the manger with him and be cared for by Mary and Joseph. Some tiny detail of creation becomes a visible sign of God's grace: a special bird comes regularly to the feeder; the smell of fresh bread invigorates my walk to work; somebody sends me a cartoon that makes me feel special, noticed, and enjoyed. Little things help me know I am baptized into the family of God.

In spring, I am tender . . . fresh . . . new.

In spring, God is protective . . . generous . . . promising.

Summer Call

A springtime faith is a good beginning for new growth, but it cannot sustain the fullness of our adult potential. The call to act independently and to claim who "I am" marks the summer season of friendship with God, as well as with humans. If we try to hold on to the spring image of God as a loving father or mother, we can expect to be pushed out of the nest, forced to fly. That is good parenting.

Naomi's summer relationship with God began when their food source dried up, and she let go of the nurturing support that had been provided for them. She dreamed a daring scheme for Ruth to undertake, risking everything to find a place for both of them with Boaz, a place where they would be treated with kindness and respect, as people instead of property. Naomi made a summer decision of determined will and then had to discipline herself to wait for results.

Ruth's summer relationship with God began as she chose to follow Naomi's instruction, to prepare for her initiate's task, and to approach Boaz with her specific request instead of simply receiving his freely given attention. Ruth apparently trusted her internal sense of timing and the external field of God's presence for support in her solitary mission. She claimed the power of her whole person—

body/spirit, language, and relationships—to confront danger and ask for what she wanted.

The scent of danger surrounded Ruth and Boaz as they met each other on the threshing floor as individuals, equally valued by God in their vulnerability and strength. They were able to move beyond the circle of conventional behavior when Boaz did not tell her what to do, but asked "Who are you?" When Ruth asked him to risk his reputation by circumventing the traditional pattern of inheritance, Boaz responded from his vulnerability: his age and his loneliness. Boaz embodied God's love and justice for the two women, opening the closed circle of Mosaic Law.

A summer friendship with God will feel the same for us: testing, challenging, stretching. The shift from spring is first marked by our need for something more than the comfort. We begin to hunger and thirst after something more than physical food. Summer is a season of change, of entering alien territory and risking life itself for some larger goal. Like Naomi, we may be forced into it by external events. Like Ruth, we meet God face-to-face in the darkness, finding both name and mission—a place in God's story that is uniquely ours—and discovering the presence of God beyond the laws of society. God lays a claim on our souls.

A summer relationship with God calls us beyond the known patterns of family and community to be creators of new structures in society. It is the season of Pentecost and mission. We develop a nagging sense of unrest and look for a special task that is uniquely ours. The dynamic tension between claiming one's self and relating to others keeps our summer friendship with God on edge, stretching, reaching for excellence, or testing the limits that served as safe boundaries before. We may experience God as distant, directive, hard to please. Like the encounter between Ruth and Boaz on the threshing floor, a summer friendship with God may contain hunger, fear, or danger—and also hold the potential for redemption of what the world says is lost.

In succeeding summers, our call may deepen into radical change of views toward institutional and cultural religion, or a passion for social justice and prophetic vision. We leave the safety of spring provision, forced by changing circumstances or simply by an internal readiness for challenge and independence. We seek new vision, new call, a change in the present order. We dare to act in new ways, to create new forms of justice and mercy in response to God's timing and internal gifts. Ideas and images materialize out of our solitary needs and give us courage to speak for others who have no voice.

We can confront the powers that would make us conform to traditional patterns and together fight for a better future. If we can welcome summer friends as those who quicken us to a larger vision for life, then we, too, can experience redemption—individual and corporate. Just as Ruth's action became part of God's ongoing story, our efforts can become part of God's redeeming activity among humans on behalf of the outcasts, the marginal, the Ruths in our midst.

As the season of "call," summer fits my Calvinist soul. I like to puzzle over God's call to vocation, examine my gifts, find a need, and go for it. I like to work and to risk: It makes me feel competent and capable. I feel the urgency of God's vision for justice behind a dream that I have carried for a long time: that every church would put a sheltering wing around some specific vulnerable group as a way to develop the souls of its members (not to "solve" our social problems).

A summer relationship with God feels natural to me, as though the purpose of life is work, duty, and reforming society. But I know that working hard gives me the illusion of control, of being able to earn God's approval. I need the balance of the other seasons to keep from being a solitary, nagging political critic. As the season of persistence and determination, discipline and focus, summer impels me to write and re-write. I wish for more flair and creativity, but often keep too busy for the playful activities that would encourage my imagination. In summer, I claim my gifts for interpretation, giving form and substance to things that others vaguely feel.

In summer, I am restless . . . eager . . . searching.

In summer, God is probing . . . calling me to explore . . . inciting me to risk.

Autumn Incorporation

Although the relationship between Boaz and Ruth broke the cultural desire for racial purity, and the relationship between Naomi and Ruth made the role of women's friendship more visible, the interpretive role of the community was essential for creating a new image of God's intention: redeeming the role of women and women's friendship in the language of story. The community's autumn relationship with God was celebrative and inclusive. According to their covenant tradition, the community itself was an expression of God's purpose in that time and place.

Autumn friendship with God is rapidly disappearing from American culture. Fewer and fewer people find community in a church, and other kinds of civic associations are giving way to private and personal pursuits. Spiritual seekers are more drawn to meditation or making a solo vision quest in the desert, not the ongoing demands of a collective body. In our individualistic culture, autumn is a difficult season for meaningful friendship with God.

A covenant community—one called into relationship by God—is the primary form of human relationship with God in both Hebrew and Christian Scripture. Jesus called it the Kingdom of God, where table fellowship was open to everyone, especially the lost, the least, and the lonely. People cared for one another. Worship reenacted the primary biblical stories of Exodus, Exile, Redemption, and Resurrection. A close-knit community lived out its understanding of God.

But the reality of such community has largely disappeared from our culture. We move like interchangeable parts and wonder why we feel so adrift, so unsatisfied. Younger people seem to stay attached to their parents longer, fearful of casting loose into the chaotic sea of materialism that marks our culture. Older people cluster in retirement homes so they will not "bother" their children. Churches struggle to engage the spiritual dimension of our lives. We are tempted to substitute television action or Internet chat rooms for real relationships.

In spite of our apparent independence, we still need to find some small community, a mystical body where we are known and loved, in which to explore the diversity of God's intention for human life. A chosen family can help us diversify from the norms of society and, at the same time, provide security within the known conventions of communal life. Within a community, we can relax the exclusiveness of springtime pairings and expand the boundaries of family to include other casual—and intense—relationships from summer and winter. We can move from thinking in singularities to working in the broader functions of "our" life together. In belonging to a community, we can also face the truth that we are all outcasts, strangers, even outlaws. We can glimpse the rich tapestry of creation and recognize our need for others.

In a sacred community, we can expand our sense of purpose and belonging, share stories of how life is and how it ought to be, and catch sight of how memory and imagination can make life fun and interesting. Living with different generations can help us face our individual limitations of time and space, death and diminishment. Community rituals can call us beyond the present and steep unconscious forces in an elixir of hope and resurrection. In community we can develop a longer timeframe and participate in God's ongoing redemptive purposes, even when we doubt the importance of our individual contribution. In community, we can experience the symphony of God with all the nuances of tone and harmony, rhythm and silence.

My autumn relationship with God is focused at Seekers Church. Worship is central and grounded in prayer. Our weekly worship is very participatory: Different people preach and offer the liturgy. We look to the life of Jesus, and we listen a lot for the Spirit's guidance. We spend a good deal of time working with our gifts and the needs of people around us, challenging each other, as Frederick Buechner does in *The Hungering Dark*, to consider where our deep gladness meets the world's deep need.

Our monthly Stewards' meeting gives the core group time to make decisions about our inward and outward journey together. We also gather for playing—monthly sing-alongs, dancing, camping trips, play readings, art projects, and celebrative meals. Together, we know that God is less concerned with efficiency than faithfulness. Together, we

remember to watch for the widows and orphans, the sick and impris-
oned at the edges of our community. Together, we have rituals and litur-
gies that shape our common life in the direction of God's love. When I
am with Seekers, I can let go of the terrifying finiteness of my personal
life and enjoy the ongoing flow of lives that are linked in God's unfolding story of friendship with human beings.

> *In autumn, I am stretched . . . surprised . . . awed by the diversity of community.*

> *In autumn, God is multiple and diverse . . . revealing new dimensions of whole-*
> *ness—male and female.*

The Spiral Path Continues

The lives of Naomi and Ruth leave the center stage of the biblical story
in spring, with the birth of Obed. But the men and women of
Bethlehem extend the story, integrating the child into the story of their
past through Tamar, Rachel, and Leah, and into their future through the
genealogy of King David—and of Jesus. The genealogies stretch the
story of Naomi and Ruth over time, describing a path in human history,
carrying an Easter message of new life brought about by two women
who dared to break through the covenantal restrictions and bear witness
to a God of love and relationship.

As with the story of Naomi and Ruth, God extends our story,
meeting us in every season, wherever we are, internally and externally. We have different types of friendships in each season, for balance and growth, for resolution and redemption, but the growth does
not stop with the end of each season. While the path of seasons may
be understood as stages of growth and development, the seasons continue to cycle by in a spiral, repeating the process and renewing us
each time, building on the discoveries and relationships from the
previous seasons.

The story of Naomi and Ruth—two women daring to claim their
place among the covenant people—gives visibility to the creative image

of God. If God is love, and we are made in the image of God, then learning how to love is the purpose of creation. Life is for loving, and the pattern of friendships is the ongoing experience of God's loving spirit among us.

For Personal Reflection

Winter Gestation

- How would you describe a time of winter relationship with God?
- What activities have nurtured, or might nurture, your winter friendship with God?
- What have you discovered about yourself and about God in different winter seasons?

Spring Encounter

- Where do you feel sheltered by God?
- How do you experience God playfully?
- Where do you feel challenged toward birthing?

Summer Call

- How do you experience God as a summer friend?
- How do you identify your "call" or vocation right now? Is your call different from the work you do for income?
- What risk or danger has been or will be required in pursuit of your call?

Autumn Incorporation

- Where do you experience an autumn relationship with God?
- What makes an autumn community experience satisfying and/or disappointing for you?
- What would you like to see happen in an autumn community? What can you imagine might be your role in making it happen?

For a Group

(*90 minutes*)

For this closing session, have a vase of flowers on the altar cloth so that each person can take one as a symbol of the beauty (and transitory nature) of friendship. Lay four symbols on the corners of the cloth to represent the four seasons (such as a pine cone for winter, a nest of eggs for spring, flowers for summer, and a basket of fruit for autumn).

Call the circle together. Light a candle and begin with a prayer or chant. Then read the poem at the beginning of this chapter.

Staying together as a group, invite people to respond to this question: *"Which season best describes your relationship with God right now?"*

Invite each person to place her symbol of divine presence on the altar in the appropriate quadrant, taking a slightly longer time of sharing than they have done before.

Invite people to name their discoveries about "Seasons of Friendship" during the past eight sessions.

Invite each person to take a flower with her as a symbol of friendship with God as she leaves.

Then close with prayer and extinguish the candle.

Notes

Invitation
1. John L. McKenzie, S. J., *Dictionary of the Bible*.
2. Carole Rayburn, "Three Women from Moab," in *Spinning a Sacred Yarn: Women Speak from the Bible*.

Chapter 1, The Circle of Seasons
3. S. E. Taylor, L. C. Klein, B. P. Lewis, T. L. Gruenewald, R. A. R. Gurung, and J. A. Updegraff. "Female Responses to Stress: Tend and Befriend, Not Fight or Flight," *Psychology Review* 107(3):41-429.

Chapter 2, Winter Friendship: Finding Myself
4. Joan Chittister, *The Story of Ruth*, 43.

Chapter 4, Summer Friendship: Searching for Call and Identity
5. Robert L. Hubbard, *The Book of Ruth*, 50-51.
6. Joan Chittister, *The Story of Ruth*, 69
7. Ellen Goodman and Patricia O'Brien, *I Know Just What You Mean*, 18.
8. Judith Duerk, *Circle of Stones*, 19.

Bibliography

Bridges, William. *Transitions: Making Sense of Life's Changes.* Reading, Mass.: Addison-Wesley Publishing Company, Inc., 1980.

Buechner, Frederick. *The Hungering Dark.* New York: Seabury Press, 1981.

Chernin, Kim. *The Hungry Self: Women, Eating & Identity.* New York: Times Books, 1985.

Chittister, Joan D. *The Story of Ruth: Twelve Moments in Every Woman's Life.* Grand Rapids, Mich.: William B. Eerdmans Publishing Co., 2000.

Duerk, Judith. *Circle of Stones: Woman's Journey to Herself.* Maui, Hawaii: Inner Ocean Publishing, 1989, 2004.

Eichenbaum, Luise, and Susie Orbach. *What Do Women Want: Exploding the Myth of Dependency.* New York: Berkley Books, 1983.

Fiorenza, Elisabeth Schussler. *In Memory of Her: A Feminist Theological Reconstruction of Christian Origins.* New York: Crossroad, 1983.

Goodman, Ellen, and Patricia O'Brien. *I Know Just What You Mean: The Power of Friendship in Women's Lives.* New York: Simon & Schuster, 2000.

Hubbard, Robert L., Jr. *The Book of Ruth.* Grand Rapids, Mich.: William B. Eerdmans Publishing Co., 1988.

Koppelman, Susan, ed.. *Between Mothers & Daughters: Stories Across a Generation.* New York: The Feminist Press of the City University of New York, 1985.

Linafelt, Tod. "Ruth." In *Studies in Hebrew Narrative & Poetry (Berit Olam Series),* Edited by David W. Cotter. Collegeville, Minn.: The Liturgical Press, 1999.

McKenzie, John L., S. J. *Dictionary of the Bible.* New York: Macmillan Publishing Co., Inc., 1965.

Morton, Nelle. *The Journey Is Home.* Boston: Beacon Press, 1985.

Rayburn, Carole, A. "Three Women from Moab." In *Spinning a Sacred Yarn: Women Speak from the Pulpit* by Ann Patrick and Sister Ware. New York: Pilgrim Press, 1982.

Rubin, Lillian B. *Just Friends: The Role of Friendship in Our Lives.* New York: Harper & Row, Publishers, 1985.

Russell, Letty M., ed.. *Feminist Interpretation of the Bible.* Philadelphia: Westminster Press, 1985.

Sanford, John A. *The Invisible Partners: How the Male and Female in Each of Us Affects Our Relationships.* New York: Paulist Press, 1980.

Sheehy, Sandy. *Connecting: The Enduring Power of Female Friendship.* New York: William Morrow (HarperCollins), 2000.

Spencer, Anita. *Seasons: Women's Search for Self through Life's Stages.* New York: Paulist Press, 1982.

Trible, Phyllis. *God and the Rhetoric of Sexuality.* Philadelphia: Fortress Press, 1978.

Woodman, Marion. *Conscious Femininity.* Toronto, Canada: Inner City Books, 1993.

Woodman, Marion, and Elinor Dickson. *Dancing in the Flames: The Dark Goddess in the Transformation of Consciousness.* Boston: Shambhala, 1997.

About the Author

Marjory Zoet Bankson is an artist, author, and relational teacher. A popular speaker and workshop leader, Marjory has been the keynoter for national meetings of Presbyterians, Episcopalians, American Baptists, United Methodists, Church of the Brethren, and Mennonites. Currently the editor of *Faith@Work* magazine, she previously served as the president of Faith@Work between 1985 and 2001. Faith@Work is a resource for relational ministry in daily life, assisting personal and institutional renewal through the magazine, relational events, and leadership training.

A graduate of Radcliffe College (Harvard University) in government and economics, Marjory has a master's degree in American history from the University of Alaska and an honorary doctorate from Virginia Theological Seminary, where she has been cited for her work in lay ministry. She has also taught high school history in Alaska, served as the first women's counselor at Dartmouth College, and worked as a professional potter, while exploring the classical spiritual disciplines of silence, journaling, simplicity, and service.

Marjory is a Steward at Seekers, a Church of the Saviour community, where she preaches and teaches regularly. Her books include *The Call to the Soul: Six Stages of Spiritual Development; Seasons of Friendship: Naomi and Ruth as a Model for Relationship;* and *Braided Streams: Esther and a Woman's Way of Growing* (all from Augsburg Books).

The Banksons have been married more than forty years and make their home in Alexandria, Virginia.

The Call to the Soul by Marjory Zoet Bankson
192 pages, 0-8066-9035-6

Each major life transition gives us a chance, Bankson proposes, "to name what we are here for." Using mythical archetypes, biblical and personal stories, she presents a revealing six-stage soulwork cycle to help us find our calling. A valuable resource for people seeking to nurture their spiritual growth, individually, in groups, or with a spiritual director.

Braided Streams: Esther and a Woman's Way of Growing
by Marjory Zoet Bankson
190 pages, 0-8066-9036-4

Explores Queen Esther's story as a model for integrating the spiritual, vocational, and sexual streams of life.

Spiritual Lemons: Biblical Women, Irreverent Laughter, and Righteous Rage
by Lyn Brakeman
128 pages, 0-8066-9015-1

Brakeman explores the passions of biblical women, such as Sarah's laughter, Jephthah's daughter's anger, and Martha's envy. Each of the eight chapters probes what these women might have felt and encourages women to name and claim their feelings.

The God Between Us: A Spirituality of Relationships by Lyn Brakeman
1460 pages, 0-8066-9037-2

Using the lively lens of midrash to revisit biblical stories—where people notoriously had their share of disconnections with each other and with God—Brakeman imaginatively uncovers the mysterious ways God is present in all our relationships. Includes commentary and questions for reflection or discussion at the end of each chapter that adds a rich dimension for individual or group use.

Available wherever books are sold.